RETIRING First Class

CLINT COMBS & LARRY BRADSHAW

Clint Combs

Clint Combs received his bachelor's degree from the University of Houston in Houston, Texas. For over twenty years, his extensive experience as a financial consultant in investments, life insurance, property and casualty insurance, personal and family budgeting, estate planning, financial planning, and Federal and State taxation has given him international recognition. He holds the designation of Registered Securities Representative.

He is the co-author of two other books: *Rich On Any Income* and *Rich On Any Allowance*.

Mr. Combs is most noted for his Rich On Any Income International Seminars that have been successfully taught to thousands of people and corporations. Retiring First Class has been added into his seminar system and seminars on this vital financial subject also are offered.

He is the father of seven children. Sean, Slade, Cody and Tamas make up the boys, while Kristin, Kariena, and Ancusta make up the girls. Ancusta and Tamas are adopted children from Romania. Ancusta is a beautiful dark-eyed gypsy Romanian daughter and Tamas is a handsome blond-haired, blue-eyed Russian and Romanian boy.

Clint likes to read, body build, and help people solve their monetary problems.

As he states, "My whole life has been dedicated to helping people financially. It is really quite satisfying to watch people who have nothing follow our financial principles and become financially independent. Like I always tell them, it's not what you make, its what you keep through budgeting and investing wisely that makes the difference."

J. Larry Bradshaw

Mr. J. Larry Bradshaw combines his extensive financial planning experience with his interest in helping others in *Retiring First Class*. A financial consultant and Qualified Retirement Plans Coordinator at the investment firm of Smith Barney Shearson in Salt Lake City, Utah, he is also a consultant for several qualified retirement plans in the Intermountain West. In addition to being licensed in twenty states for securities, commodities, futures trading, life insurance and annuity sales, he holds a Utah State license as a Registered Investment Advisor. His responsibilities at SBS include financial consulting and coordinating office activities on retirement plans and the company's consulting services.

His background includes thirty years in the construction and materials distribution businesses, which included fifteen years in local real estate development and construction.

He was elected president of the Board of Education of the Granite, Utah School District, and founded the Excel Foundation, a non-profit organization dedicated to recognizing and financially rewarding outstanding public school educators. He has served as chairman of the Granite Education Foundation, and has long been active in Rotary International, Kiwanis, and Scouting leadership.

He is a lifelong Scouter himself, and has been awarded the Silver Beehive and Silver Beaver for service to Scouting.

He served in the U.S. Army and is an alumnus of the University of Utah, where he graduated with a Business (Marketing) degree. He and his wife, Patricia, have six children.

First Printing: July 1993

International Standard Book Number
0-88290-470-1

Horizon Publishers' Catalog and Order Number
2050

Printed and distributed
in the United States of America by

Horizon
Publishers
& Distributors, Incorporated
50 South 500 West • P.O. Box 490
Bountiful, Utah 84011-0490

Contents

1

In The Beginning

"Plan for retirement? Give me a break! We boat on the weekend, golf during the week; I'll spend my money now and have great memories when I'm retired."

Retirement! That's 35 years away. I just wish I could get my hands on that retirement plan money at the company. I want it now, not when I'm down the road.

"Me? A single parent think of retirement? I live from paycheck to paycheck. I never have enough money to go around. No matter how much money I make or how many raises I get, there is always some emergency that eats my increase in pay. I need it now not later!"

A wise old sage once expressed, *"It ain't what's here that's scary, its what's a comin'."*

Our plane had been part of a forty-five-minute traffic jam waiting for take-off clearance. While waiting impatiently, we discussed what went on behind those mysterious closed curtains which separated coach from first class seating. Once airborne, we could hear the tinkling of silverware and the muted voices of people who seemed to be having a good time. "Is this possible, passengers actually having a good time on an airplane?" In those days, airlines felt little concern about the comfort of tall passengers who sat sandwiched into the no leg-room seats—seats designed for occupants under five-foot-nine inches in height and not over thirty-six inches around the girth.

The person to the side of us was the unlucky passenger assigned to the center of a triad of seats beside a person who was far to wide for the seat. Normally this isn't too much of a concern but on our flight this person was also left handed.

No sooner had he lowered his service tray to receive the tightly compacted food servings, than the passenger in front of him lowered his recliner chair to its "back yard Saturday afternoon" position, tightly wedging the tray against his knees, and forcing him firmly against the seat back. I knew this was a test for astronaut training. If he passed his six hour flight test in this position, he could be considered for the moon mission.

The flight attendant hurriedly dropped meal trays before us. Our left-handed friend immediately began attacking his provisions. His left elbow routinely jabbed the right arm of his row companion. It was apparent that if enjoying the luxury of eating on this moon cruise were to be realized, the row companion would need the patience of Job and the timing of a Symphony Conductor. We intently watched the left handed "Ninja" with knife in his left hand and fork in his right, pointing the weapons at his mid section. He held an endangered morsel of chicken with his fork and began sawing away. Only now did I fully realize why some people were created left handed. It was so they could occupy aisle seats on the right side of a Boeing 707 during meal time. Problem! This overweight passenger obviously received the wrong seat assignment.

We began to study the situation and observed the acute angle of the row companion's left hand. "If he can just twist his hand to the opposite angle as lefty, and time the motions of his right arm in counterpoint to the rhythm of the intruding left elbow, this awkward right-hand-to-left-hand challenge might be overcome.

In spite of all the meticulous geometric calculations and allowances, he missed his mouth. Glancing quickly at his beautiful wife, seated quietly at his left side, we spotted the remains of the broccoli spear dangling from his fork. The buds from the head of the broccoli added a master artist's touch to the right shoulder of her cashmere sweater. She looked at the pathetic decoration on her shoulder. "Rather creative, don't you think?" he hesitatingly queried of her.

The thought came to us, "One of these days, wouldn't it be great to try traveling first class? Must we be destined to travel coach class throughout our life, even in our retirement years?"

Settling down, I drifted into a dream of extra-wide cushioned seats of the first class cabin, . . . stretching my legs and enjoying the heated, lemon-scent towels offered by the stewardess, . . . freshening faces, cleansing hands and enjoying the crisp white cloth covering the lowered trays. Fine china and real silverware! Not the "mini type" but a full-length knife, fork and spoon glistening on a linen cloth. Imagine! No "shrink pak" plastic sealed around the silverware. No struggle to get the plastic sack removed from between the tines of the fork before eating. Ah' This is the life.

Retiring! Real retiring! Golf, tennis, travel, and all of the other activities one does at the end of a lifetime of dedicated service. Dreamy Hawaiian music in the background . . . enticingly fragrant blossoms, . . . drink in the beauty of the rolling waves of Waikiki Beach breaking over the crystal white sand . . . .

Terror! Will we be condemned to retire in coach or economy class after all these years of hard work? Would the beach, waves, soft sand, dancers, flower lei's, and dreamy music of first class-retirement ever be ours?

"Back to your coach seat Buddy!"

"No! Not more eating with crossed and tangled arms! Anything but that. We deserve better than coach! It just isn't fair!"

"Sorry. Forty-five years times coach fare equals coach retirement. It's just simple arithmetic."

"I'll try harder. I'll plan better. I'll . . . "

"Sir? Sir! Would you straighten your seat back and fasten your seat belt? We're preparing to land."

"Whew! It was only a dream—or was it a nightmare of the Ghost of Retirement Yet to Come"?

Laughing at my dream became commonplace. Yet, it has become the catalyst for our continuing commitment to . . . RETIRING FIRST CLASS!!

2

Common Sense
And Proper Planning

As most of us know, "People rarely plan to fail, ... They just fail to plan."

Remember: You can have everything in life you want, including first class retirement—if you plan for it properly, with enough lead time and work.

Let's look at some real-life examples of how spending habits, use of credit, distinguishing needs from wants, and budgeting affect retirement plans.

You Cain't Get There From Here

Have you ever been hopelessly lost and totally frustrated in unfamiliar territory, stopped and asked directions and had the local store owner tell you, "You cain't get there from here"? The same quote occasionally fits for those who wait too long to begin their retirement planning.

A famous phrase, one never out of date is, "The longest journey starts with a single step."

Some common problems encountered in those first steps to retirement planning are:

1. lack of timely planning,
2. lack of patience to allow investments to work,
3. unrealistic expectations for the future value of money, and
4. total dependence on Social Security for retirement.

The Spending Binge

Paul lived high, his entire life. All of his friends looked upon him with envy. "Great athlete," "talented," and "handsome," were common comments from those who knew him. His job always seemed to provide plenty of cash. Even in high school he drove expensive cars and a four-wheel-drive truck. On weekends you would find Paul at the mountain mud hole enjoying his 4x4 vehicle. He always spent freely on his dates. It wasn't uncommon to hear him say, "It doesn't get any better than this!" His motto? "The biggest and the best." As he progressed in years he would say, "With inflation high and going higher, I'll be paying back cheap dollars by the time my loans come due."

There was never a thought of saving, either for emergencies or retirement. Paul met Penny and their courtship was one continual spending binge, which convinced Penny that he was Mr. Fantastic. Soon Paul and Penny met the minister. After their marriage, in addition to the normal adjustments to married life, they had more than their share of marital difficulties. Most of the conflicts were centered around finances. After a few years, Penny decided to establish some independence and budget wisdom, and sent Paul packing on his spendaholic way.

As for Paul, time and money just seemed to slip away from him. He felt positive his income would always grow with the inflation rate; and, as for retirement? "Well . . . with my Social Security and the money I'll save those last few years, I'll get by just fine. Everything I want to do will have been done by then, so I won't need much retirement money."

It's a good thing Paul doesn't plan on doing much after retirement! Starting to plan for retirement at age 60, after a lifetime habit of spending more than he earned, will require some major changes in life style.

"Where did all the years and money go?"

The Fable Of The Plastic Rich

Nick always bought what he wanted. If the money wasn't there
he used his backup finance program. You guessed it—"The fantastic
plastic"—more commonly known as the charge card. It never occurred
to Nick, the same stalwart of the community who walked the marble
corridors of the Bank of England in the Disney movie *Mary Poppins,*
and encouraged the young visitor of the bank to, "deposit tu'pence
in the bank," could be the local banker who charges him 18% interest
on his charge card balance; while he, with the stern face of integrity,
pays Nick a skimpy 3% on his meager-passbook balance.

Like Paul, the pathway of Nick's first marriage had been a very
rocky trail. Visits with financial consultants and marriage counselors
had not changed Nick's reliance on credit for the solution to all his
wants and desires which, for so many years, had been disguised as
needs. Nick's first marriage ended in divorce, but fortunately he
recently found Nancy. Nancy thought trying to pay for a marriage
license with plastic money demonstrated the most creative finance
idea she had ever seen.

Times hadn't changed for Nick. Something sparked fantastic about
plastic. Nancy began to develop the attitude, " . . . something drastic
needed to happen to the fantastic plastic." One evening Nancy lovingly
encouraged Nick to join her in a budget session."Nick, we're not
getting any younger. We have about fifteen years to prepare for our
retirement. Don't you think we should develop some sort of a plan?"

"If we had just part of the interest I've paid over the years, we
could retire anytime," Nick sadly lamented. "I wonder how much
we will need to put away for the next 15 years to be able to live comfortably when we retire?

Nancy counseled, "Nick, I think its time we reviewed the real cost
of credit card purchases. In his entire lifetime, my dad never once
paid interest, rest his soul. He always said he paid himself instead
of the bank. I never fully understood what he meant until I looked
at our expenses and found the interest we paid last year probably
would have funded a retirement plan."

Our wise old sage speaks again! *"Them's that understands interest collects it. Them's that don't, pays it."*

Needs Or Wants

Ralph got a rather late reservation for the most economically priced fare to first-class-retirement; even so, he still had 25-years to work a plan. If he diligently pursued his ability to save $4,000 each year, it may work.

Throughout most of their lives, he and his wife Carol thought budgeting was a real pain in the posterior. Their budget never seemed to work. He would see a desireable item in a store and be immediately convinced it would fill a need for something or other. Then, in a passionate fit of perceived need . . . he would succumb, . . . and buy.

More than once, Ralph's inability to distinguish needs from wants put him at odds with the little lady, take, for example, the time he passed the local Gun Shoppe. The banner on the store front beckoned Ralph inside: GIGANTIC GUN SALE. "Well, I'll just go in and browse around," he thought. As he left the store with the new 12-gauge over-&-under dream gun tucked under his arm, he began to think of his rationalizations for buying it. Arriving home, he thought he would have a little fun and see if he could throw the, commander off guard. "Now let's see, the verbiage and tone of voice are going to be very important. 'Carol, I have a confession to make. I've done this terrible thing.'" That should divert her attention long enough to tell her how much he loved her before presenting the one tool for his collection of hunting paraphernalia that certainly would make him successful in next year's pheasant hunt.

When he recited his well-rehearsed lines to her, she immediately saw through the smoke screen and said, "You bought a new shotgun!" He was taken back at her ability to read his mind.

"After all, the family does need to eat! Why did she get so upset about a little $500 shotgun? I need that gun!" he rationalized.

Their home was a museum of perceived needs Ralph had collected over the years. Although Carol also enjoyed hunting, she knew one day the passion for hunting would fade and their lives would be more centered on security for the future; not on keeping the freezer stocked with meat from the "hunt." Carol bit her tongue as she worried about their retirement. This time it was too much! That old familiar thought went through her mind again. "The only difference between men and boys is the price of their toys. Boys need toys; men just think they do."

It was time for some drastic action. After the long overdue strategy session, Carol took control of the check book, cancelled all but one of their credit cards and began allocating spending money according to their new budget allowance.

Thou Shalt Not Touch!

Lisa wasn't tight-fisted with her money. She just appreciated how hard she worked to earn it. She decided that at the young age of 35, and being a single parent, she would need to make prudent plans for the future if she hoped to provide Jamie and Kimberly with the benefits of a secure, loving, comfortable home and a college education. She knew the advantages of budgeting and the power of earning tax-deferred interest. If she could earn interest on the portion of her savings which usually went to pay taxes, she would compound her ability to increase wealth. She had to be frugal. "Making it on your own isn't always easy. What are the possibilities?" she pondered. "The easiest? . . . . Budget for the future and . . . establish an IRA account. Two advantages are definitely better than one." Not only did this allow her to plan or future needs, but her strategy incorporated the tax deferred compounding effect on her earnings. She was able to subtract $2,000, each year, from her tax return as an allowable IRA deduction.

Lisa knew the government was serious about the purpose of IRA's being for retirement when they placed a 10% excise tax in addition to ordinary income tax, on early withdrawals from the IRA.

She found there were a few other tax-advantaged places to stow some shekels now and then. She decided that in addition to her IRA deposit of $2,000 per year, she would begin to build an investment portfolio. She learned about high-quality tax free municipal bonds and tax deferred annuities.

By putting an additional $1,000 in these investments every year, Lisa will provide for the future needs of her children and build a retirement account to supplement her Social Security. In the years when expenses are down, the house and car are paid for, the kids are educated and on their own, Lisa will live very comfortably and her dream of world travel can be realized.

The House With The Golden Windows

When Will was a young boy, his mother read him the fable of "The House With the Golden Windows." He promptly forgot the moral of this ageless story, but, it was re-created in his mind every sunset evening as he looked toward the foothills above his home and saw the golden hues of summer sunset shining upon the windows. Each night he recommitted himself to "own a house with golden windows."

In his small notebook, Will recorded his allowance, errand income, and the money he earned selling cards. Then he made his deposits into each of the small baby food jars his wise mother had helped him prepare as his personal budget system. He knew when the jar for spending was empty, he had no more spending money available until his next income. He learned even more about saving and budgeting when he completed his Merit Badge in Personal Money Management while progressing toward his Eagle Award in Boy Scouts.

He understood the concept of, "Thou shalt not touch thy savings account, for in the day that thou doest, thou shalt foul up thy educational opportunities." His dedicated mother impressed upon him the wise counsel, "Don't put off saving. Your life can be wonderful when your finances are secure."

When Will was twenty-five years old he finished college, having paid for it from his college budget account. He married his college sweetheart Sue and accepted his first full-time job. The pay was modest, but Will appreciated the opportunity to put into practice all the knowledge he had studied and sacrificed for during his college years. Sometimes, as their lives unfolded, it was very difficult to save. Having four children presented a challenge to his budgeting skills, but his lifetime habits of saving five to ten percent of everything he earned, and of budgeting for future needs, allowed him to accomplish his goals. The more he disciplined himself to "do it," the stronger his desire became, until budgeting for savings became common place. "As my salary grows," he thought, "I can increase my savings to $2,000 annually or even more.''

Imagine, saving as little as $100 per month and creating a sizeable estate. Now at forty years his preparation of $1,200 per year totaled $48,000; however, the compound effect of this investment together with its yield over 40 years had increased his retirement account to nearly $220,000 by just "doing it." He never tried to make a "killing" on his invested money. His "serious money," (retirement account) was always well diversified and invested in safe investments.

Will made several other investments and, over the years took some moderate risk, because he was looking for a higher yield; but, in the retirement account his second great commandment helped him amass a small fortune. "Thou shalt protect thy capital and invest it for thy home with Golden Windows!"

As he grew and matured, he realized his "Home With Golden Windows" was the security he developed over the years. Through this knowledge he controlled his financial destiny. He was in debt to no one. However, his spiritual debt to his Mother for the blessings of hard work, frugality, gratitude and humility with which he had been endowed ran deeply.

Its Never Too Late To Start

Lon personified all the traits of "You cain't get there from here." His life had been one continual hand-to-mouth lack-of-planning race track. The construction industry, with its perpetual up-and-down cycles coupled with winter slowdowns, much needed truck and tool repairs, and compounded by problems collecting his accounts receivable, were always Lon's justification for not having any money.

Now, with just five years until his desired retirement date he delivered $50,000 to us. It was his inheritance from the estate of his parents. At retirement to supplement his Social Security, he wanted to begin withdrawing $5,000 per year and not reduce the principle of his investment.

We recognized five years did not allow sufficient time for him to take much of a risk posture. We made some conservative projections for him.

To facilitate this withdrawal request Lon would need to earn 14% each year on his initial $50,000 investment, if he were to preserve his capital. He also needed to average this return throughout the remainder of his life to enable him to withdraw $5,000 per year in after-tax dollars.

What are the chances of investing with a guaranteed return of 14% and no risk of loss? If you thought little or none, you are right on the mark.

Assuming a realistic 7-8% return, we began projecting his $5,000 annual withdrawal. His inheritance would last until he reached age 74. The year following his 74th birthday showed $2,186 remaining in his investment account. We hoped that Lon had paid his self-employment tax for the previous 40 years in business. If he does not have the maximum Social Security benefit when he retires at age 65 it will be a very lean retirement. Lon loved the out-of-doors, but at this moment he was not a "Happy Camper." He found that retirement without adequate funds is a juggling act, and very difficult to perfect when you are over sixty years of age.

What are the alternatives?

- Reduce annual expenditures?
- Increase income?
- Take the risk of less-safe investments to get higher returns, recognizing the possibility of losing some principle before it begins returning the sought-after high rates of return?
- Go to Las Vegas for an all-or-none investment program?
- Work until age seventy and begin budgeting now for retirement?

Lon had been led astray! At age 25 his life expectancy was another half century; however, at age 60 he could expect to live for an additional quarter century. His early projections, made in terms of parts of centuries, seemed so far in the future. "My how time flies when you're havin' fun"—especially the fun of spending all you earn.

Unfortunately, Lon was scheduled for a budget class trip through retirement. He may even need to travel "stand by" while waiting for another miracle. He thought his inheritance would be his first-class ticket, but lack of proper planning had bumped him to economy class, or possibly to the baggage compartment.

The secret to gauging where you are going is to carefully assess where you are and where you have been.

Many of these financial adventures are based around the cliché of being "hopelessly lost but making good time." You cannot build a successful retirement program looking through a rear-view mirror. The past, however, is an excellent measuring guide to assess where you are and where you want to be.

Lets look ahead at your greatest financial habit.

3

Your Greatest Financial Habit

Members of the average American family, as indicated in a past article, spend 123% more than they earn. This implies if a person makes $20,000 a year, he is spending $24,600. Where is the additional $4,600 coming from? You guessed it, *debt!*

Can you imagine working an average of 40 to 50 hours per week for approximately 50 weeks of the year totaling 2,000 to 2,500 hours, to have the privilege of spending more than you earn? Multiply $4,600, the overspending, by the number of years one works in a life time; if the overspending habit remains uncorrected, a staggering financial headache may result. Unfortunately, aspirin won't take away this problem, only the results one produces can.

Frequently people ask us, "What's the first step to a financially sound retirement?" The answer is simple, though sometimes tough to accomplish.

We believe the first step in retiring first class is to acquire the skills necessary to live within your income and save 10% per month for the rest of your financial life.

What are the skills necessary to live within your income? How do you save 10% of your gross income per month?

Basic Budgeting Steps

There are simple budgeting steps that will enable you to live within your income *within the next ninety days.* Yes, you are not misreading. If you accomplish these budgeting skills, you will be living within your income within three months and saving money too! Here are the simple and easy steps:

Step One: Calculate your net spendable monthly income for next year. Subtract from your gross monthly income all your deductions for taxes, insurance, and other deductions you may have. The remainder is your net monthly spendable income.

Step Two: Determine your last year's spending for major categories. Collect and add all your cash receipts, credit card receipts, and any other expense receipts you may have for the last year, and categorize them into your past spending categories. You may be able to do this by analyzing your checkbook register. Once you've determined the total in each category for the last year, divide each category by 12 to get your average monthly expenditure in each category for the last year.

Step Three: To determine what you are going to spend in the next 12 months use your last year's expenditures calculated in step two. For example, let's say you spent $300 per month for food. In this step examine the $300, your past food category expenditure, and consider increasing it by a reasonable percentage to allow for inflation of food prices and/or the increase in the size of your family. With these thoughts in mind, you might estimate your projected food budget at $325 per month for the next year. Projecting what you are going to spend for the next 12 months based upon what you have spent in the previous 12-month period will give you greater accuracy for each spending category.

Step Four: Add all the categorized amounts you are going to spend monthly for the next year. Compare the answer to your net spendable monthly income in step one. If your outgo will exceed your income, review your *fixed expenses, variable expenses,* and *recreation & entertainment expenses.*

Your *fixed expenses* are those you are legally obligated to pay. These legal expenses in most cases cannot be reduced. However, you may want to consult with your lender to reduce your monthly payments in order to make your out go equal your income. Most often lenders are happy to do so except for home loans where in order to reduce the payment, the entire home loan may need to be refinanced. Otherwise, you should be OK.

Your *variable expenses* are those over which you have complete control. Some of these expenses would be food, clothing, and gifts. These expenses can easily be reduced.

Your *recreational & entertainment expenses* may be some of the highest. Review these carefully and reduce where you feel you can.

From our experience of over a decade of financial counseling, people can bring their income and out go in line most often by doing this simple little task. Then re-add the budget-category amounts and you should be right in line with your net spendable monthly income.

Step Five: Divide the budget categories between husband and wife if you are married. If you are single or a single parent, you get to manage all the budget categories yourself. A checking account for each spouse will make it a little easier to manage your spending categories. Once again, if you are single or a single parent, you only need one checking account.

These easy and simple budgeting steps will start you on your way to living within your income in just 90 days. If you need additional budgeting help see the appendix of our book, *Rich On Any Income.*

How To Save Every Month

Now let's shift gears and address the issue of how to save 10% of your gross income every month. Living within your income paves the way for the next step: acquiring the knowledge and skills necessary to save ten percent of your gross income each month for the rest of your life.

Many people acquire what we call a "put-n' take savings account." A "put n' take savings account" allows them to deposit money on Monday and withdraw it on Friday for their wild weekend of fun.

Why do we do such things? Our financial common sense tell us that, our greed gland must be reckoned with sooner or later, which resembles a famous oil filter commercial that ends by expressing, "You can pay me now or pay me later."

We find people generally desire to save money; however, they lack the knowledge and skills, *not the money.*

Many years ago, someone proclaimed, *"You can eat an elephant if you do it a bite at a time."* If you apply his principle to saving, it will read like this, "You *can* save your hard-earned dollars if you do it a 'percent bite' at a time." We refer to this as the *Elephant Theory of Saving.*

The *Elephant Theory of Saving* is simply this: After you are living within your income, you should begin saving 1% of your gross monthly income each month until you feel comfortable with that amount. Then you should increase it to 2%. Then 3%. Then 4%. Then 5%. Then 6%. Then 7%. Then 8%. Then 9%, and finally 10%. Ten percent of your gross income is all you ever need to save.

From our experience, people occasionally try to jump from 2% to 8%. That big a percent bite may choke your saving goals. Don't skip from a small percentage to a large one. Take it a "percent bite" at a time, and you will be immediately successful.

We find from counseling people about living within their income and using the Elephant Theory of Saving, that it builds confidence. And more importantly, it builds your bank account and ultimately your retirement. Finally, it gives you the successful feeling of saving your money. These savings, properly invested, will grow into a nice nest egg for a great retirement. Retirement then becomes a reality— not a wish.

A letter from a couple related, "When you told us about living within our income and using the Elephant Theory of Saving, we chuckled. It sounded cute, but would it really work? We decided to try it and to our amazement, it does work. If we can live within our income and save money, anyone can. Thanks."

The reality of this issue is, *you can do it.* Visualize yourself living within your income and saving money every day, every week, every month, every year. "Whatever the mind sees and believes, it will succeed in achieving." To the mind, reality and imaginary are the same . . . reality. When you live within your income and use the

Elephant Theory of Saving, you will succeed every time! See it, believe it, and you will do it!

You now have acquired the knowledge and skills of the two most important steps in securing your retirement:

1. live within your income.
2. save 10% of your gross income.

Once you live within your income and save 10% of your gross monthly income by using the Elephant Theory of Saving, you will *guarantee yourself a happy and a financially 'worryfree' retirement.* You can provide a good retirement for yourself without giving up the good life now. So *plan it and do it.*

In the next chapter, we will be discussing the best economic friends for your savings.

4

Compound Interest: Your Best Economic Friend

We were conducting a seminar for a group of especially talented young people. They were from several areas of the United States. Their talent: making money. They were attending a special financial seminar on the stock market and other financial information.

We were asked to speak to them on managing their money. We presented the following example of how your best economic friend can be of benefit to you.

We asked, "How many of you would like to be millionaires?" Needless to say all raised their hands. Their comments were, "I don't believe it." "What's the catch?" "It's impossible!" "What's the gimmick?"

The story unfolded. "Do you know who your best ecomomic friend is?" we asked. One person replied, "The California Lottery." All the students had a good laugh. We rephrased the question, "Besides the lottery and your rich uncle, who is your best economic friend?" This time the class of 250 students was silent.

"The answer," we replied to their curious minds, is COMPOUND-ED INTEREST. After a few boos and pretended paper wad throwing, they exclaimed the answer was too simple. We continued, "Here's a riddle: what financial work horse never sleeps? It can kill you financially and also make you rich." This time there was a gleam in their eyes as if to say, "You may have something here." One perceptive teenager raised her hand proclaiming, "Interest! Debt Interest can kill you while you sleep; compounded interest income can make you rich at the same time!"

"You are absolutely right!"

"Let's illustrate how to become millionaires. Who in the class is 12 years old?" Some raised their hands. "Is anyone 21 years old?" No response. "All of you are qualified to become millionaires," we observed. By this time note pads and pencils were in position for taking notes.

"Here is the key," we started. "How many people in this room know what IRA stands for?" Many hands shot upward. The general response indicated it was the Individual Retirement Account nicknamed the IRA, which permits one to deduct from earned income, $2,000 per year for retirement, thereby saving federal income taxes.

We had their attention. "If you saved $2,000 each year from age 21 to 28, how much would you have saved?" "Sixteen thousand dollars," someone shouted. "That's right. If you let that $2,000 per year grow, tax deferred, from ages 21 through 28 at 7% compounded interest, how much would you have accumulated?" The class was busy calculating the answer. Three people simultaneously shouted, "The answer is $21,956. That's not a million," they stated.

"You're right. But see how compounded interest is working for you."

"Where is the million dollars?" the class demanded.

"Hold on."

"Oh sure! Here comes the catch," one snickered.

"There's no catch. Let's take another example. If you saved $2,000 a year for eight years, you are beginning to build the millionaire habit. Here's a problem. Are you ready?" The looks on their faces reminded us of race car drivers at the starting line of the Indy 500.

"The question, is if you saved $2,000 each year from age 21 to 65 at 7% interest, how much would you have tucked away?"

You could see the flurry of activity as they rushed to see who would get the answer first. A young man with hand waving wildly screamed, "$532,242." "No way," another shouted. "The answer is, . . ." the class grew quiet as the all-star football player from Texas arose and said, "$611,504. Where's the million?" His expression reminded us of the television commercial showing the lady peering at her hamburger rather sheepishly, as she groaned, "Where's the beef?"

"You are getting close," we responded.

"Do you see how compounded interest is helping you attain millionare status? Let's continue. Saving $2,000 a year from 21 to 65 at 10% interest totals how much?"

In a few seconds, a quiet young man in the class cautiously responded, "Is it $1,305,282?" "Yes," we applauded. "That means," he continued, "that means, when I do it, I'll be a millionaire!" The class was getting the same answer. The singing chants began in the classroom, "I'm a millionaire, I'm a millionaire."

One student asked, "If this is so easy, why doesn't everyone do it?"

The question was so timely, we thought she had read our script. "Because they don't understand the principle of compounded interest, or they would. The later you start your IRA working with compounded interest, the more money it takes to become a millionaire, so start early and be a guaranteed millionaire when you retire."

"When you qualify for an Individual Retirement Account (IRA) and save $2,000 a year, you can usually deduct it from your earned income, thus saving federal income taxes. More importantly, the interest on your IRA savings grows tax deferred. This means the interest on your money is allowed to accumulate without paying federal or state tax on it, so your financial principle increases faster and faster. The higher the interest rate, the faster you gain millionaire status."

After the calculations, they still found it hard to believe. "The principles you have been taught today are true. Whether you exercise them or not, is up to you.

"In our example when you deposited $2,000 a year for eight years at 7%, your IRA grew to nearly $22,000 when your deposits totaled only $16,000. When you calculated millionaire status, a surprising financial fact was discovered. Remember when you calculated the value of depositing $2,000 a year from age 21 to 65 at 10%? The answer was over one million dollars. The real issue is not the one

million dollars, but the fact you only needed to deposit $88,000—
$2,000 a year for 44-years to become a guaranteed millionaire."

Their financial minds were going into overdrive.

"Don't, don't, focus on the one million dollars; focus on the
investment principle of compounded interest. Your $88,000 returns
$1,305,282!" When the idea connected, they began to applaud. Then
they cheered. They understood when they master the skills of saving
money, their financial future will take care of itself.

"Once you understand the rule of compounded interest and make
it work for you, you to can have financial security. Compounded
interest doesn't ever sleep. At every tick of the clock, it works for
you. While you are on your vacation, it works for you. While you
are sick, it works for you. It works 24 hours a day, seven days a week,
365 days a year for the rest of your life.

Seeing their smiling faces was compensation enough. We knew
that they knew compounded interest was the very best financial friend.

As we stated earlier, "*Them that understands it, collects it. Them
that don't, pays it.*"

That class of young people really learned and understood the great
financial principle of compounded interest, don't you agree? What
were your thoughts as you read this story about compounded interest?

The George Thomas Financial Rule

We are tuned in with your thoughts: "I'm not 12, I'm 45. What
do I do about compounded interest at my age? Can it work for me?
Will I really be able to retire first class?

The answer is *yes* if you thoroughly understand the *George Thomas
Financial Rule.*

The George Thomas Financial Rule is based upon two very
successful Presidents of the United States: George Washington and
Thomas Jefferson.

George Washington, as most Americans know, was the father of
our country, besides being our first American President. Also, he
was financially successful. Today he is prominently recognized as
the father of the one-dollar bill.

Thomas Jefferson was also a President of the United States and very successful in arranging his financial affairs, and he is prominently known for being the Father of the two-dollar bill.

Realizing these historical and current facts, the George Thomas Financial Rule illustrates the use of compounded interest. As a current or future retiree, you are interested in only one idea. The idea is "dollar stretching."

"Dollar stretching" is calculating your retirement nest egg into the future so you know the amount of retirement dollars you may have and how long it will last. The goal, of course, is to have the money outlive you, not you outlive your money. As medical facts attest, you may be retired as long as you have been working or even longer. The George Thomas Financial Rule will help you accomplish this "dollar stretching" calculation.

This financial rule indicates to you how long it will take for your George Washington dollars to become Thomas Jefferson dollars. In other words, it helps you answer the question, how long will it take my invested dollar to increase from one dollar to two dollars?" You don't have to be a rocket scientist to figure out going from one dollar to two dollars is doubling your money.

The rule states simply the following: "If you invest a George Washington at 1%, it will become a Thomas Jefferson in 72 years.

The George Thomas Financial Rule relates only to doubling your money. Presidents Washington and Jefferson can be effectively used to estimate your retirement nest egg by calculating the number of years it will take to double your investment, or to determine at what percentage your investment would grow, regardless of your age and time to retirement.

Let's see how it works. To find the number of years it will take to double your money, you calculate it this way.

For example, you have 1,000 George Washingtons invested in an account paying 6% interest. If you want to know how many years it takes for them to grow to 1,000 Thomas Jeffersons, or $2,000, use this mathematical formula. As you look at figure 1, page 34, you will note we have divided 6% into 72. Your 1,000 George Washingtons will double to 1,000 Thomas Jeffersons, or $2,000, in 12 years.

How about another example? You still have 1,000 George Washingtons in the bank, but this time they are earning 8%. How long will it take the Georges to become Thomases? The answer is 9 years. How did you get that? Look at figure 2, page 34, you divided 8% into 72.

The larger the interest percentage, the less time it takes to double your principle. In our examples using $1,000, 6% took 12 years to double, while 8% only took 9 years.

One final example. Take the same 1,000 George Washingtons in your savings account. How many years will it take George to become Thomas at 10%? Your right! 7.2 years. See figure 3, page 34.

Let's use an example to calculate your retirement nest egg and give you an approximation of the money in your retirement account.

You and your wife are age 35 with two children. You have an Individual Retirement Account (IRA) worth 11,000 George Washingtons growing at 6% tax deferred. You have saved this IRA amount by living within your income and exercising the Elephant Theory of Saving. You and your wife are thinking about retirement. You feel if you had cash of $90,000 to $100,000 in your IRA fund by the time you retire, your retirement plans could be achieved.

Your children are at the age when college is a very important factor to consider. The question is, do you think you will have enough in the bank when you retire to live comfortably? Is your goal of $90,000 to $100,000 realistic? Should you divert your future contributions from your IRA, where they will grow tax deferred, into your children's taxable college fund?

What should you do? By using the George Thomas Financial Rule, you can easily answer your questions and chose between the different financial alternatives.

Once again, how many years will it take at 6% for your 11,000 Georges to become 11,000 Thomases with no further IRA deposits? (Remember to get the number of years your money will double, you divide 6% into 72 to get the answer) That's right! 12 years. In twelve years you and your wife will be 47 with $22,000 in your retirement account. If your IRA is still earning 6%, it will double in the next 12 years, so your total in your IRA when you are both 59 should be $44,000. With $44,000 in your IRA, growing at 6%, still doubling every 12 years; your retirement nest egg will be worth $88,000 at age 71! Outstanding! It isn't age 65, but you know this at age 35, not at age 65 when it may be to late. A few more deposits into your IRA account will make your retirement goal come true. You also know the goal is achievable and not a dream. You can thank George Washington and Thomas Jefferson for this vital financial knowledge.

With this information, you have the following financial options to consider: (1) not to make any future IRA deposits, or (2) continue to make the full $2,000 annual deposits as you have done, or (3) make IRA deposits of $1,200 and put the other $800 towards the future college fund for the children. Even if you reduced your annual IRA payment to $1,200 and deposited it each year or every other year until you retire, your goal of $100,000 could easily be attained, and your children could have the college education you want to provide for them.

By using the George Thomas Financial Rule, you can easily choose the best financial decision for your current situation as well as for your retirement.

Great or Greed?

Another unique characteristic of the George Thomas Financial Rule is that it tells you what the rate of return is on your investment.

Let's illustrate. One day you're reading the newspaper and see an advertisement stating, "If you let me use your money I'll double it for you in only four years." "Sounds great," you mutter to yourself.

If this investment were to double your money in four years, how could you calculate the rate of return within seconds? It is simple and easy with the George Thomas Financial Rule.

In this example take the number of years (four) and divide it into 72. The rule tells you the return percentage on your investment. Divide 4 into 72, and you get 18%! (See figure 4, page 34.)

Does it sound like a great or greedy return on your money? The George Thomas Financial Rule doesn't evaluate the risk you're taking to acquire 18%, even if you could get it.

The rule tells you instantly, however, if the return on your investment is "Dream World" or "Real World." Your common sense proclaims the following: *"If it sounds to good to be true, it is."*

Most of the time the George Thomas Financial Rule is used to determine how many years it will take for your money to double in value. By using this rule periodically, you could review the value of your retirement nest egg to insure you are on track for a great retirement.

Knowledge is *power,* and you have just learned one of the greatest wealth-building principles to add to your financial arsenal, the George Thomas Financial Rule.

You are doing great and learning fast. In the next chapter, you will learn about the Golden Stream of Income You CAN'T outlive.

Figure 1

$$\frac{72}{6\%} \ = \ 12 \quad \text{\# of years}$$

Figure 2

$$\frac{72}{8\%} \ = \ 9 \quad \text{\# of years}$$

Figure 3

$$\frac{72}{10\%} \ = \ 7.2 \quad \text{\# of years}$$

Figure 4

$$\frac{72}{4 \text{ years}} \ = \ 18\%$$

5

The Golden Stream
You Can't Outlive

Budgeting The Flow Of The Stream

Ira (or "Irey" as he was called by those who knew him well) had been the Water Master for as long as any of us could remember; at least 50 years. In the summer when the water was "in" (in the ditches) Irey could be seen on a daily basis in his overalls, denim jacket, and his seasoned western hat which had many lines of perspiration around the brow. He'd be walking the ditch banks with his well-worn irrigating shovel slung over his somewhat-stooped shoulder. The shovel seemed to routinely fall into the "shovel pocket" on his left shoulder as his arm draped over the handle forming a perfectly balanced lever. Irey always looked the same even on Sunday. He just put a tie on his plaid shirt and left his shovel in the shed instead of bringing it to church. The sight of him clearly indicated a man "who knew his business . . . water." If you needed information on any of the Culinary Water or Irrigation Systems, you went to talk with Irey.

A local contractor came into Irey's territory to begin construction of a house. The excavation had been "staked out" and the back hoe unloaded. There hadn't been a half dozen buckets of earth moved when Irey appeared out of no where. He "kinda hobbled" up to the excavator and raised his hand like a Great Indian Chief calling his nation to order.

The noise of the powerful diesel diminished as the engine wound down and the operator dismounted the huge intruder to face the Chief. Irey cautioned! "You boys be careful! The West Side Water Line goes right through here." The Contractor and operator both smiled as they confidently replied "We checked with Engineering, and we're clear."

Irey didn't say a word. He just nodded his head twice and stepped back 10 paces to watch. He placed the blade of his shovel precisely 2 feet to his front put both hands over the end of the shovel handle, drew the support end of this miraculous tripod toward his chest, and just leaned there.

The hoe operator "mounted up on ol' paint" and commenced his work. He had only moved a few more buckets of earth when the sickening sound of metal crunching against metal echoed across the lot. A tooth on the bucket of the back hoe had gouged a 2" hole in the top of a mysterious hidden high-pressure water line. The jet of water shot up diagonally, in a southeasterly direction over Irey, over the backhoe and over the County Road at the front of the lot. The operator "shut down" the hungry backhoe and dismounted as if electrocuted. The over-spray from the now cascading waterfall aided by a light summer breeze settled down over the backhoe, the contractor, the operator, the excavation, and over Irey.

Chief Irey remained motionless, not flinching or blinking as he received an unplanned pre-soak for his evening bath. He simply leaned there. His head made a slight verticle nod as he said, "Yup that's it. Be seein' you boys." He sauntered off across the lot to his more familiar ditch bank.

In addition to having the water demand for each branch of the ditch memorized, Irey knew the precise amount of water necessary each month of the year to satisfy the requirements of all the down stream water users.

He treated the available supply of water like a finely tuned budget system. He also possessed a liberal education on how leaks in the ditch bottom occur ". . . when someone gets the bright idea of re-routing a ditch." If disturbed the ditch bottom must be resealed. The normal strata of sand and rock allow too much water percolation into the ground rather than flowing the water over a silt-sealed bottom.

Irey's ditch system resembles your Golden Stream of Income. If you plan to get the optimum use of your income stream, you need to understand the significance of a potential financial leak on a carefully budgeted income flow.

To build a sound financial stream, realistic objectives must be established. These plans might include guarding against financial leaks preserving the life style you desire as well as allowing enough time before you make the great gear shift to retirement. The objectives should address the issues of what you plan to do and over what time span. After your objectives have been established, it is possible to create a plan that will accomplish these attainable goals within the desired time.

More About Compound Interest

Now that you have gained an understanding about the George Thomas Financial Rule and the beneficial effects of compound interest let's study them in a little more in detail.

When we were boys we raised animals much to the chagrin of our mother. We adopted into our family every little critter that looked like it needed a home. Turtles, hamsters, rabbits, chickens, dogs, and cats all found comfort at our house. Occasionally, some of the animals escaped from their various places of abode and made a mess of one kind or another (most often another) in the house. One day we heard the distinct sound of a Whooping Crane coming from the bedroom. We ran to welcome the new resident to our house. We were disappointed to find it was only mother announcing to the neighborhood that she found our missing hamster which made the mistake of innocently crawling across her slipper-clad foot.

In the process of our animal-raising education, we learned that, when upset for one reason or another, hens in the chicken coop would refuse to "set" on their nest. Without their warm attention to the nest eggs the eggs would not hatch and there would be no increase in the chicken population.

The same thing often happens with interest on investments. People may invest for the future yet forget to pay warm attention to the nest eggs (principle) and consequently damage the hatch (interest). Or they withdraw their earnings leaving only the principle. They may allow their immediate desires or perceived needs, to over-arch the logic of their long term plans. Their "wealth building posterity" never increases and the power of their principle diminishes as it is slowly but effectively eroded by *financial enemy: inflation.*

A common error in planning for the future is not considering the effect of inflation and taxes on your income stream.

Roy and Alison spent the major portion of their lives quietly following the tradition of their parents by depositing 10% of their gross income into their savings account. They are proud of the amount they have accumulated and rightly so.

They have been saving $100 every month. Their plan is to increase their monthly saving amount at each year end as their income grows. This is consistent with their goal of saving 10% of their income. They have assumed their income will increase at about 5% per year. If they protect the hatch (interest) as well as the principle they can watch it grow to nearly $175,000. The dollar amount seems large in terms of today's purchasing power; however after 30 years inflation it may be substantially eroded. They are pleased about their nest egg and they are confident it will last throughout their retirement when coupled with Social Security. Let's look at what their investments can be expected to accomplish over time.

Chart #1 illustrates tax rates and the present rate of interest on their savings account. The left column lists the year of comparison at five-year intervals. The center column illustrates the amount saved monthly. This amount changes each year as their income increases. The monthly deposit amount changes every year, assuming 5%-per-year annual raises in pay. The right column illustrates the year-end value at 5-year intervals.

Chart #1
Compound Values of Savings Account

1. Federal Tax Rate: 15%
2. State Tax Rate: 7%
3. Total Tax: 22%
4. Interest Rate Assumption: 4%
5. inflation assumption: no consideration for inflation
6. Projected for: 30 Years
7. Savings amount increases 5% each year

Year	Amount of Monthly Deposit	Year-End Value & Accumulated Int.
5	122.00	7,482
10	155.00	18,734
15	198.00	35,186
20	253.00	58,751
25	323.00	91,978
30	412.00	138,254
		prior to tax

Their savings account usually earns interest slightly over the 4% level, and with inflation averaging 4-6% its easy to see they are approximately breaking even. We counseled them, "There is another issue to consider. What about taxes? Your savings interest has earned a yield of 4-6% and has been subject to both Federal and State Income Taxes. You added the interest to your tax return each year and paid the necessary taxes. Let's recompute. Assume an average interest on your savings of 4%, then pay the taxes on this 4% gain. Assuming tax brackets of 15% Federal and 7% State, you actually save a little over 3% in after-tax income."

The Invisible Economic Thief

Chart #2 illustrates the real value of your savings after taxes. If $138,254 thirty years in the future is a concerning number to survive on, the real value of $122,158 after taxes are paid is even more frightening. If inflation accelerates at 4%, your dollars buy 4% fewer goods at the end of each year than at the beginning. Or stated differently you must have 4% more money to buy the same amount of goods and services. This inflation is as real as any expense in your budget. It is so often overlooked because it is the "invisible economic thief." It must be treated as any other expense. If it is overlooked there will be a severe standard of living adjustment at retirement time!

Chart #2
Compound Values of Savings Account

1. Federal Tax Rate: 15%
2. State Tax Rate: 7%
3. Total Tax: 22%
4. Interest-Rate Assumption: 4% Projected for 30 years
5. Effect of taxes: After deducting taxes the new yield is 3.16% (4% interest on savings minus 22% Taxes)
6. Inflation assumption: no consideration for inflation
7. Savings amount increases 5% each year

Year	Amount of Monthly Deposit	After-tax Year-End Value & Accumulated Int.
5	122.00	7,295
10	155.00	17,896
15	198.00	32,942
20	253.00	53,930
25	323.00	82,817
30	412.00	122,158 after tax

What is the impact of inflation and taxes? Let's look at a graph of what inflation does to your income stream.

Chart 3
Investment Returns Required
to Maintain the Purchasing
Power of Investments
under various inflation and tax rates

Tax Rate	Inflation rate%										
	1	2	3	4	6	7	8	9	10	11	12
15%	1.2	3.4	3.5	4.7	7.1	8.2	9.6	10.5	11.8	12.9	14.1
20%	1.3	2.5	3.8	5.0	7.5	8.7	10.0	11.2	12.5	13.7	15.0
25%	1.3	2.7	4.0	5.3	6.0	9.3	10.7	12.0	13.3	14.7	16.0
30%	1.4	2.9	4.3	5.7	8.6	10.1	11.4	12.9	14.3	15.7	17.1
35%	1.5	3.1	4.6	6.2	9.2	10.8	12.3	13.8	15.4	16.9	18.5
40%	1.7	3.3	4.9	6.6	10.0	11.7	13.3	15.0	16.1	18.3	20.2

At my currrent ____% tax bracket and ____% projected rate of inflation, I will need to earn ____% as a taxable investment to just break even on my investments.

Notice the inflation rates at the top of the graph and the tax rates at the left side. Using the graph like a multiplication table, find your rate or return in the body of the graph. For example, if you are in the 15% tax bracket for Federal Taxes and the 7% bracket for State Taxes, find the row on the left column that approximates most closely the total of these two taxes, or 22%. In this case the nearest number is 20%. Let's assume an anticipated inflation rate of 6%. Reading across on the 20% tax bracket line to the 6% inflation rate column you find 7.5%. This is the yield or rate of return you'll need to maintain the purchasing power of your retirement dollars.

Somewhat frightening, isn't it?

Chart #4 shows the real rate of return as Roy and Alison lose 1% of their purchasing power. They may faithfully "put away" nearly $80,000 over 30 years, only to find their purchasing power will buy the goods that could have been purchased for around $70,000 when they began their saving program. Yes, without proper planning and use of financial tools, they may fall behind 1%, after 30 years of frugality.

Chart #4
Real income after taxes and inflation

1. Federal Tax Rate: 15%
2. State Tax Rate: 7%
3. Total Tax: 22%
4. Interest Rate Assumption: 4% projected for 30 years
5. Effect of taxes: after deducting taxes the new yield is 3.16% (4% Interest on savings minus 22% Taxes)
6. Inflation Assumption: Inflation rate is projected at 4¼% (Purchasing power loss 1.09% annually)
7. Savings amount increases 5% each year

Year	Amount of Monthly Deposit	Year-End Value & Accumulated Int.
5	122.00	6,425
10	155.00	14,286
15	198.00	23,995
20	253.00	36,082
25	323.00	51,220
30	412.00	70,265

after taxes and inflation

Total deposits = $79,757
Future purchasing power = $70,265
Loss of purchasing power = $ 9,492

Compounding Interest Tax Deferred

You have seen the positive effect of compound interest. Now let's see what happens if you add the power of deferring taxes.

Roy recited his admirable creed to us: "I've always paid my bills, including my taxes, right on time! I'd just as soon get the taxes out of the way and not have them hanging over my head."

But we said, "Roy, lets compare the compounding of interest, which you have practiced, to a similar investment where taxes are deferred until the 30th year. Go back and review the total account value of Chart #1!

Your Retirement account grew to nearly $140,000. Now go back and compare this to Chart #2 which considered the payment of taxes each year.

This chart showed that taxes cut the real yield on the account to just over 3%. Now let's compare the net values of using tax-deferred accounts versus paying taxes yearly on the same income stream.

Chart 5
Comparison of tax deferred and taxed yearly income

	Tax Deferred	Taxed Yearly
Total invested:	$ 79,757	$ 79,757
Future Value:	$138,254	$122,158 taxes paid
Taxable gain:	58,497	42,401
Combined Taxes 22%:	12,254	taxes paid
Total Gain after tax:	46,213	65,000
Add back initial investment:	79,757	79,757
Total account value:	$125,970	$122,158 after tax
Additional gain after taxes:	3,812	--

This consideration assumes a lump-sum withdrawal which may cause your tax rate to increase. We realize under normal circumstances you would not do that; therefore, this chart is a worst-case scenario. But even with this worst-case assumption, by delaying the payment of taxes until withdrawal, your net gain after tax will be approximately $3,800 greater.

The reason it makes such a dramatic difference in the end result is this: not having to pay taxes yearly allows you to earn income on the portion you would normally pay as taxes.

Needless to say, Roy and Alison were somewhat taken back by the difference in spendable money for the same $79,757 investment by deferring the payment of taxes. This additional amount can be used to assist them in retiring first class.

Our discussion continued, "All of our comparisons have used your established goals of monthly savings amount, and existing rate of return using the passbook savings account as your investment choice. In a few moments we will discuss other investment options to increase your return and still preserve the low risk nature of your investment objectives."

They smiled at each other as Roy commented, "We really could give our retirement a boost by taking advantage of tax deferral. How can we benefit from this principle now when we're just a few years short of retirement? We've already paid some taxes to Uncle Sam. Is there any hope for us, starting at this late date?"

Roy, Alison, remember the adage, 'The longest journey starts with a single step.' Even though you have some of your retirement account secure, it's never too late to take advantage of the power of tax-deferred or tax-free compounded interest."

Tax Deferral Vehicles

Let's review some basic financial vehicles that allow you to defer taxes and increase your rate of interest:

IRA Accounts:

You can deposit up to $2,000 per individual per year into an account which not only allows your income to compound tax deferred, but also allows your $2,000 deposit to be deducted from your income. There are some limits on the deductibility of the deposit amount, but those affect relatively few people. Everyone should explore the IRA possibilities. A non-working spouse may also deposit up to $250 into an IRA account. This is referred to as a spousal IRA.

Pension, Profit-Sharing and Keogh (self-employed) Retirement Plans:

These plans are excellent vehicles to attain a more enjoyable retirement, if you are fortunate enough to have an employer who has adopted one. Many forward-thinking employers have adopted profit sharing or pension plans to assist dedicated employees with their retirement. The funding for these plans is a contribution from the employer. Profit-sharing plans are funded by employer contributions from either current-year earnings, past (retained) earnings, or they can be funded as any other business expense of a company, regardless of the amount of current or past profits.

Self-employed individuals are also eligible to adopt retirement plans. Frequently the type plan they adopt will be referred to as a Keogh (or self-employed) Retirement Plan, named after the Federal Legislator who sponsored the bill to introduce this great issue into law.

To qualify for a Keogh retirement plan, a business must not be incorporated. The owners of the business may make contributions to their Keogh plan by depositing up to 15% (25% under certain circumstances) of their annual income, not to exceed $30,000 per year.

If the owner has employees who have been employed for over one year, the owner is required to make retirement deposits for all of his employees who meet eligibility requirements. The deposit percentage for employees must be the same percentage of income as the deposit made in favor of the owners. For example, if the owner defers 10% of his income into his Keogh retirement account, he must also deposit 10% of the income for all eligible employees for their benefit.

Pension plans differ from profit sharing plans in that they are a guarantee by the employer at your retirement date, (established by the plan document) to pay a guaranteed amount for the rest of your life or for a fixed number of years.

Company 401(k) Income Deferral Plans

If your employer has adopted a profit sharing 401(k) salary-deferral plan, you may elect to defer up to 25% of your income into a 401(k) retirement account. This deferral has a maximum amount which indexes each year for inflation. The amount was $7,000 in 1986. This amount is also a deduction from your taxable income, as well as allowing for the compounding effect of interest, tax-deferred. Some employers may chose to match a portion of your deferral with company dollars. The total of employee deferral and company match may not exceed the annual contribution amount established by law.

Tax-Deferred Annuities

Most of us are acquainted with insured certificates of deposit (C.D.'s). A tax-deferred annuity is similar to a C.D. except it is issued by an insurance company, and the interest earned is not subject to taxation until withdrawal. A more aggressive investor may choose a variable annuity. This resembles a tax-deferred mutual fund.

Tax-Free Income

It sounds too good to be true doesn't it? Tax-free interest rates are not as high as taxable interest, but when you study the net result of eliminating taxes on income, it makes a significant difference. Let's look at why this "too good to be true" idea works.

Interest earned on most bonds issued by municipalities, (cities, towns, counties, states, etc.) is exempt from taxation by the federal government. With some exceptions, interest on municipal debt (tax-free municipal bonds) may also be exempt from state taxes. Depending on the interest rate for alternative investments, "muni bonds," as they are affectionately referred to by those who own them, may put substantially more spendable cash in your pocket than taxable interest alternatives.

Assuming a yield of only 4% on a tax free bond (many bonds have substantially higher yields than this), compare *Chart #1* (add the assumption, "tax-free income Muni Bonds") with a similar investment with taxable income, as listed in *Chart #2*. After saving for 30 years, would you rather have $138,000 or $122,000 as the reward for your diligence?

If you would have saved your money in a tax-free investment, you would have increased your in pocket cash by this $16,000 amount.

Let's couple these principles of tax deferral and tax-free income with some techniques in the next chapter that put these principles to work. The issues are (1) risk and reward, (2) allocation of assets, (3) diversification, and then we will discuss choices for safety in retirement investing.

6

Your Investment Pyramid

The Principles Of Risk vs Reward

We conducted a retirement seminar in a small community, known for its relatively high population of retired people. After brief exchanges and get-acquainted statements, we asked,"What are the components you would like to see in the ideal investment?" As we expected, this group replied astutely. They named: safety, tax advantage, yield, liquidity. and estate advantage. We then asked about their risk tolerance level. One gentleman in the audience volunteered, "I want no risk! I just will not put my assets at the whim of an uncertain market." We were pleased at his comment.

Preservation of capital is *Rule #1.*

We then asked this same gentleman, "What return would you like to receive on this risk-free investment?" He pondered for a minute and then responded, "Well . . . I'm not greedy. Probably seventeen, eighteen, or twenty percent."

We smiled internally but, discovered a conflict of terms. It was a lead-in to . . .

Rule #2.

High return and no risk are at opposing ends of the investment scale.

The pyramids of Egypt were not only symbols of wealth and power, religious shrines, and final resting places for royalty; they also were designed to be eternal. They were not tall slender obelisks; they had a solid, broad base-demonstrating a strength no earthly force could damage or destroy.

Rule #3.

You don't build pyramids from the top down.

The Pyramids stand today as a testament to the wisdom of this planning. Retirement plans should be constructed with much the same meticulous fore-thought and design. On the bottom of your investment pyramid, we recommend a solid foundation of wealth. Equity in a home, all forms of insurance protection, certificates of deposit (insured savings), tax deferred annuities, treasury securities; money-market funds and cash are investments that form this broad, solid base. (see figure #1)

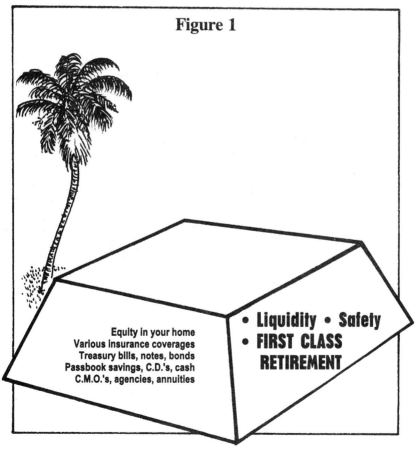

Figure 1

Equity in your home
Various insurance coverages
Treasury bills, notes, bonds
Passbook savings, C.D.'s, cash
C.M.O.'s, agencies, annuities

• Liquidity • Safety
• FIRST CLASS
RETIREMENT

As you ascend your pyramid of financial success, the degree of risk increases slightly as you add utility stocks, blue chip stocks, preferred stocks, high grade corporate and municipal bonds, conservative mutual funds, variable annuities, and investment real estate. (see figure #2)

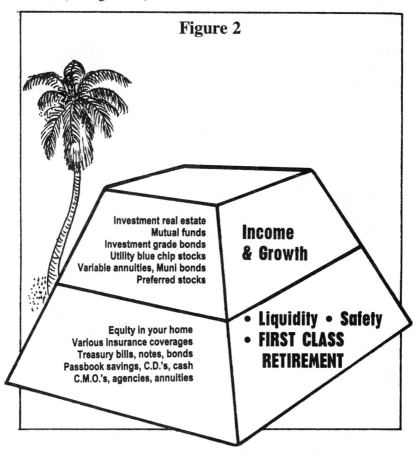

Figure 2

Investment real estate
Mutual funds
Investment grade bonds
Utility blue chip stocks
Variable annuities, Muni bonds
Preferred stocks

Income & Growth

Equity in your home
Various insurance coverages
Treasury bills, notes, bonds
Passbook savings, C.D.'s, cash
C.M.O.'s, agencies, annuities

• **Liquidity** • **Safety**
• **FIRST CLASS RETIREMENT**

The third level of your pyramid may be the addition of speculative common stocks, lower-quality municipal and corporate bonds, and raw land. (see figure #3)

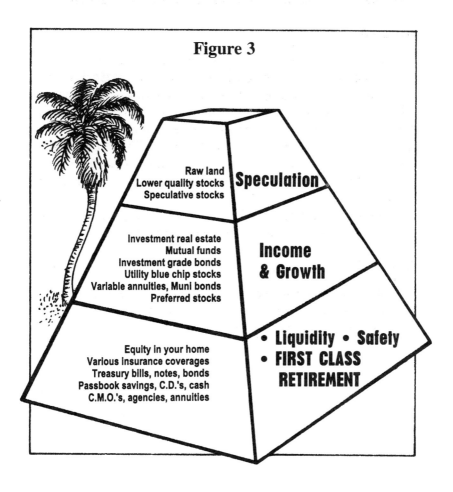

Figure 3

Raw land
Lower quality stocks
Speculative stocks
Speculation

Investment real estate
Mutual funds
Investment grade bonds
Utility blue chip stocks
Variable annuities, Muni bonds
Preferred stocks
Income & Growth

Equity in your home
Various insurance coverages
Treasury bills, notes, bonds
Passbook savings, C.D.'s, cash
C.M.O.'s, agencies, annuities
• Liquidity • Safety
• FIRST CLASS RETIREMENT

The pinnacle of the pyramid is where more risk oriented investments such as futures, option contracts and commodities belong. Most of us never get to this area of investing. It is the area you only participate in if you can afford to lose money. (see figure #4)

Rule #4

If you can't afford to lose it, don't gamble with it; invest it.

You frequently hear about the person who received ten times his money in 7 days trading option contracts. You don't often hear the other side of the story. This same investor may have lost 20 times before he made his "big 10-times-the-money winner." This is a very specialized area of investing. If a profit is to be realized from trading options, it requires nerves of steel, some cash to gamble which you can afford to lose, and a very skilled, experienced investment counselor.

A sample investment pyramid may be helpful as you evaluate the construction stage of your personal investment pyramid.

Rule #5

If you don't understand the investment, and you don't want to take time to learn about it, or you don't have a skilled trusted financial consultant to assist you, don't do it!

Figure 4
YOUR INVESTMENT PYRAMID

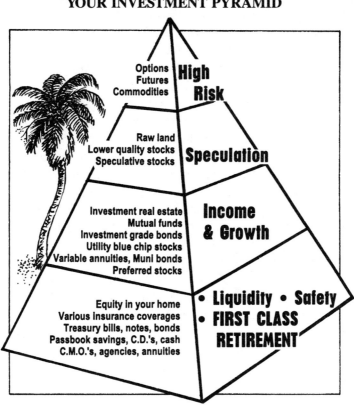

An investment can be anything from a can, buried in the back yard, to futures and option contracts. The real issue is, "Can you manage the risk and still reap the reward?"

Allocation Of Money Between Investments

Planning for your financial future may occasionally require a little exploratory work; indeed, major surgery may be necessary to get your financial future on the mend.

We often muse at how differently the recommendations of professionals are treated. You go to your doctor for an evaluation. The doctor examines you, analyzes the problem and says, "Stop all heavy lifting, walk a mile a day, take 2 Norgesic Tablets daily, and it *should* clear up your back problem."

Do you ever tell the doctor, "No. I don't like to walk, and I can't stand Norgesic. What else have you got?"

No! You do what the doc' tells you to do, while knowing he doesn't have a 100% cure ratio and, that's totally acceptable to you, isn't it?

On the other hand, you may go to a financial consultant for an analysis of your financial health. He makes a recommendation after establishing objectives and a time frame. You tell him, "Let me think about it, and I'll get back to you in a while." Right? You may tend to look for some perceived "safe harbor" while pondering the cure, and yet, sometimes the consultant's analysis and recommendations are as crucial to your financial well being as open-heart surgery is to a doctor's heart patient.

It is appropriate to develop the same degree of trust in your financial surgeon that you have in your medical surgeon. Neither have a 100% success ratio, but hopefully, both have been selected because of the high degree of trust you have developed in them and in their abilities. If the trust isn't there, take time to find out why. Is it because you have told the financial doctor the diagnosis before you allowed him or her to put their expertise to work in your behalf? Is there some basic philosophical difference between you and the financial consultant? Has the consultant established proper investment objectives with you? If the opinion of the consultant and his recommendation does not fit your objectives, look for a new consultant that will develop objectives with you and work toward your realization of them.

In today's investment world, there is a program available to many people in which a professional, who manages large amounts of money and securities (portfolios) for major corporations and pension plans, also works through some of the prominent brokerage houses to manage money for smaller clients. They are called Professional Money Managers. The brokerage firm becomes the liaison between you and the money manager (this simplifies life for the manager), and the firm is willing to deviate from its established policy of only managing portfolios of several million dollars. Most of the professional money managers have their investment style scrutinized by many talented individuals as well as investment analysts. Rarely is a money manager found that has developed a successful system for investing, whether it be a system for stocks, bonds or a combination of both, who is confident enough in the system that he will place 100% of a fund in a selected investment. Most often the money manager will allocate a percentage of the assets to an offsetting investment. For example, a stock (equity) manager usually allocates a portion of the available funds to Treasury Bills, or possibly keeps a portion in Money Market Funds. This process of determining how much to invest and how much to keep liquid is called *asset allocation*.

After reviewing these concepts with Roy and Alison we continued, "Roy, Alison, as much as we admire your frugality, which allowed the accumulation of your wealth by disciplining yourselves to save 10% of your gross income, you could increase your purchasing power and outpace inflation by allocating a portion of your assets between other conservative investments.

The following chart illustrates the impact on your retirement account, at one percent increments added to your return on investment. Using the same figures previously established for monthly saving and the length of time for your plan to work, notice the difference in ending investment value for each 1% increase in yield.

4%	$138,254	as illustrated
5%	$161,094	
6%	$188,810	
7%	$222,544	
8%	$263,709	
9%	$314,061	
10%	$375,777	

Let's look at a possible allocation of your investments. It shouldn't be hard to increase your yield over the present 4% and still keep your portfolio on the safe side.

Asset Allocation Scale

The
Allocation of Assets

INVESTMENT
PYRAMID

FOR YOUR
RETIREMENT ACCOUNT
ASSET ALLOCATION SCALE

Total
Retirement Account

| STOCKS | TREASURIES | CASH | MUNI BONDS | REAL ESTATE | CORPORATE BONDS | ANNUITIES |

Let's assume a few guidelines. First, the scale must be in balance at all times. Second, the value of the right balance of the scale represents all the ingots (total value) of your retirement account.

The allocation process consists of changing the mix on the left side while maintaining a balance with the right side. For example: If you have 15 ingots on the right side, you must have 15 ingots on the left side. However, the choice of the ingots or the left side may be made up of any mix which consider market conditions and your investment objectives. This is where both common sense and a skilled financial consultant may come to your aid.

In the illustration, the allocation is made up of 3 ingots of municipal bonds, 4 of stocks, 2 of corporate bonds, 1 ingot of cash, 3 ingots of treasuries, 1 of tax-deferred annuity, and 1 ingot of real estate. There may be other types of financial ingots that are appropriate for your financial plan. These are just seven of the many possibilities. There may be times when no ingots of stocks, bonds or real estate appear on your allocation scale. Financial consultants and investment advisors counsel with you to help you determine a proper allocation (mix). This keeps the golden stream flowing downstream to your retirement account pool.

Diversification Of Investments

As you learned about asset allocation, you also learned some of the basic principles of diversification. Asset allocation deals with the percentage of your investment portfolio that is allocated between stocks (equities), fixed income (bonds), and cash equivalents (money market accounts), real estate, or other appropriate investment choices. Diversification spreads the risk between several different investments within each of these categories. For example, if the forecast for stocks (equities) is very positive, you may decide to allocate 60% of your investments to stocks, though you would not put all that money into one stock. Even if it was your favorite automobile manufacturer, the largest in the world, which had paid dividends for 50 years and raised its dividends for the past 30 years; you would still say, "Great" I want 10 more companies in various industries just like that one, and I will invest 10% of my equity allocation into each of these 10 companies."

The same philosophy applies to the allocation you establish for fixed income (bonds, C.D.'s, etc.). You may feel bonds of your local power and light company are the most credit-worthy investment available. Your investment allocation may call for 30% of your portfolio to be in fixed-income investments. This 30% should be diversified over perhaps seven issues. You decide to invest around 15-16% of your fixed income allocation to this utility bond issue. You are in control of your money and your retirement. You and your financial consultant decide what would be the safest financial route for you to travel.

The following graphs illustrate another important principle of asset allocation, the volatility of a portfolio with different asset mixes. Volatility is the change in perceived value by those who would invest in various assets. This change in perceived value is what we refer to as *market price*. The market price of securities may be *stable* (small or no price swings) or it may be *volatile* (significant price swings).

Notice that a typical portfolio of 100% stocks (equities) over the past 10 years has had volatility ranging from 22% gain to 25% loss (4th quarter 1987, see graph #1). If the portfolio had been diversified with 20% bonds and 80% equities as illustrated in graph #2 the volatility range would have been reduced to 18% gain and 17% loss. Notice in graph #3, a mix of 80% bonds and 20% stocks has much less voiatility (about 11% on the positive side and 4% on the negative side).

Does this mean you should cut volatility as much as possible? Only if you want the average return reduced accordingly.

GRAPH #1

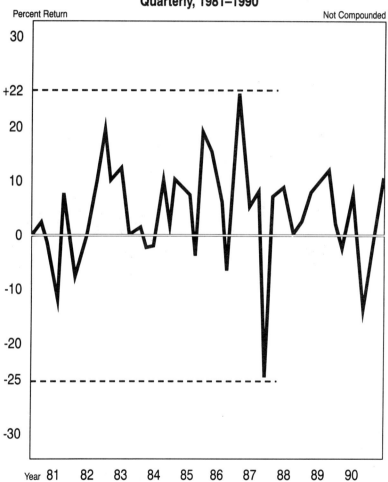

PORTFOLIO VOLATILITY
100% Equities
Quarterly, 1981–1990

NOTE: Equities reflect S&P 500; bonds reflect SLB Government / Corporate Intermediate Index

GRAPH #2

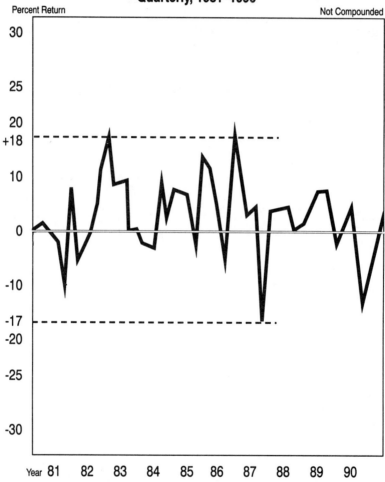

PORTFOLIO VOLATILITY
80% Equities / 20% Bonds
Quarterly, 1981–1990

NOTE: Equities reflect S&P 500; bonds reflect SLB Government / Corporate Intermediate Index

GRAPH #3

PORTFOLIO VOLATILITY
20% Equities / 80% Bonds
Quarterly, 1981–1990

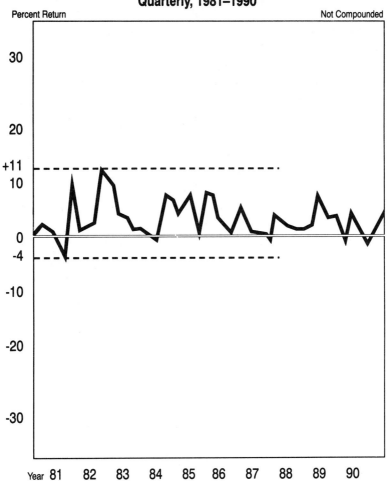

NOTE: Equities reflect S&P 500; bonds reflect SLB Government / Corporate Intermediate Index

Risk (volatility) is proportional to reward (return). Usually the higher the risk, the greater the potential for return.

A portfolio of 100% bonds with relatively low volatility may have gained a return over the past five years of 8%. A 100% equity portfolio over the same period of time may have had volatility similar to that illustrated in graph #1, approximating 20%, but may have only had a return of 15%.

The following graph, #4, shows the annualized return of various types of investments over the period of 1926 to 1990. The term small company stocks does not mean "penny stocks." It refers to small capitalization companies trading "over the counter" (OTC), also referred to as NASDAC Stocks.

Graph #5 shows how investments in stocks for the long term (five years or more) have grown to substantially higher value than fixed-income securities over the past 60-year period. The graph indicates $100 in an index fund of the S & P 500 index stocks at the beginning of 1926, prior to the crash of 1926, would have been worth over $27,000 at the end of 1985. Compare this to the value of fixed income investments over the same period of $1,227 for long-term government bonds, to $1,651 for corporate bonds. After these same numbers are adjusted for inflation the stock investment would have been $4,437 compared to fixed income investments ranging from $201 for long-term government bonds to $271 for corporate bonds. (see graph #6)

GRAPH #4
COMPARTATIVE RETURNS

Annualized, 1926 – 1990

Small Company Stocks	11.6%
Common Stocks	10.1
Long-term Government Bonds	4.6
U.S. Treasury Bills	3.7
Inflation	3.1

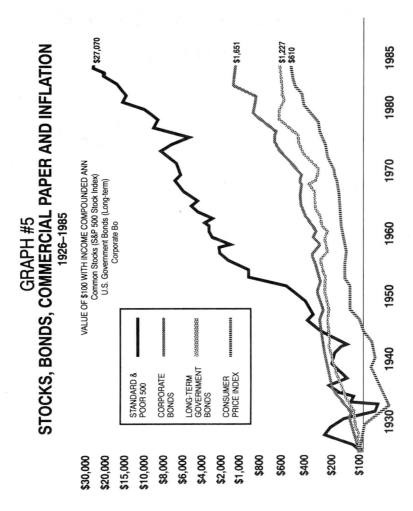

GRAPH #5
STOCKS, BONDS, COMMERCIAL PAPER AND INFLATION
1926–1985

VALUE OF $100 WITH INCOME COMPOUNDED ANN
Common Stocks (S&P 500 Stock Index)
U.S. Government Bonds (Long-term)
Corporate Bo

STANDARD &
POOR 500

CORPORATE
BONDS

LONG-TERM
GOVERNMENT
BONDS

CONSUMER
PRICE INDEX

GRAPH #6

STOCKS, BONDS AND COMMERCIAL PAPER
(adjusted for inflation)
1926–1985

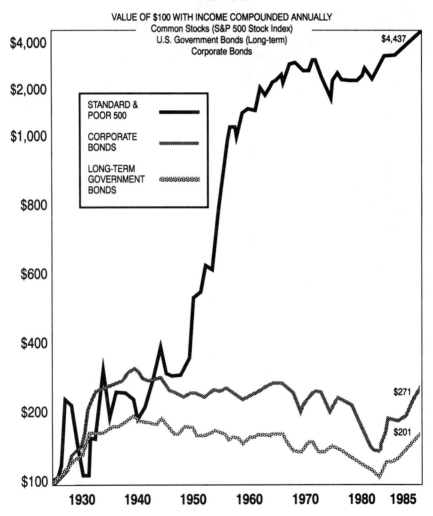

VALUE OF $100 WITH INCOME COMPOUNDED ANNUALLY
Common Stocks (S&P 500 Stock Index)
U.S. Government Bonds (Long-term)
Corporate Bonds

Do you remember Irey? He mastered the allocation of available water and knew how to budget it so all of the ditches (tributaries in city talk), contained sufficient water to feed the thirsty crops of many land owners. You need to develop these same characteristics as you plan the most effective use of your limited resources (money). If you fine tune your budget and use a little common sense about the allocation and diversification of assets, which admittedly is different for many individuals and couples, you can have the success you plan for and rightfully deserve. You will gain the respect of others, as they look with admiration at how you realized the fulfillment of your lifetime dreams, and how your diligent budgeting allows you to live the life style you have become accustomed to.

Remember! *Preservation of capital is the first rule of retirement investing.*

7

Your Top Ten Investment Parade

Now that you understand Risk/Reward, as well as Allocation and Diversification, let's look at a few investment possibilities we have affectionately referred to as our "Top 10 Hit Parade." The title obviously dates us because today it has been replaced by "The Top 10 Count Down," and tomorrow there will be some other classic title. Whatever the terminology, here they are; many you may be familiar with, some you may not. Just to be on the safe side lets describe each of our "Top Ten" briefly:

Insured Certificates of Deposit

Insured Certificates of Deposit (C.D.'s) are issued by banks and credit unions, and may also be purchased at brokerage firms. It is not uncommon to find brokerage firms offering better rates on C.D.'s than banks. Certificates of Deposit (C.D.'s) have been insured by either FSLIC (now referred to as SAIF, Savings Association Insurance Fund), or FDIC (now referred to as BIF, Bank Insurance Fund). Both of these agencies are administered by the Federal Deposit Insurance Corporation (FDIC). The government (FDIC) fully insures C.D.'s *up to* $100,000 in value for each depositor at each institution. Remember *up to,*, not over $100,000. This includes the value of the principle and accrued interest. We recommend purchasing C.D.'s for less than $100,000 per institution to allow for accrued interest. You may maintain C.D.'s at several institutions and be insured on each one, so long as each institution's C.D. value does not exceed $100,000, including accrued interest.

Brokerage firms usually act as agent for several institutions. Thus, when purchasing C.D.'s through a brokerage firm, several C.D.'s may be held in your brokerage account without violating the $100,000 limit per institution. Most often each C.D. purchased through a brokerage firm is individually insured.

Treasury Instruments

"Treasuries" are direct obligations of the United States Government. They are the ultimate in safety. It is common to find the interest rate on treasuries is less than on C.D.'s or other interest-bearing instruments. Although income on treasury instruments is subject to taxation by the federal government, they are exempt from state taxes. To figure your net yield on treasuries, you must consider the effect of the State Tax exemption. Let's look at an example of this exemption.

The numbers in the illustration are *assumptions* but they illustrate the principal.

Notice in the illustration the left numeric column (*treasuries*) shows the calculation of the net yield after deducting federal taxes on the treasury. The right column (C.D.'s) shows an 8% yield consistent with the treasury yield; however, the yield on C.D.'s is taxed by both federal and state governments. Although the yield on both instruments is the same before taxes, the after-tax yield (spendable money) on the treasuries is higher than C.D.'s bearing the same interest rate.

	Treasuries	C.D.'s
Interest Rate	8.0%	8.0%
Federal Tax Rate 15%	−1.2%	−1.2%
State Tax Rate 7%	0	−.48%
Net Yield After Tax	6.8%	6.32%

Obviously, in this case, if the interest rates are the same (which they rarely are) you would choose to invest in the treasury rather than the C.D. because your net spendable (after-tax) dollar is more.

Before you decide whether to purchase C.D.'s or treasuries, you should go through a similar exercise, comparing the "net" interest yield for each instrument. After this consideration, your treasury yield may be higher than other alternatives. If the treasury "net" yield for a similar maturity date is higher, it will be your investment choice. Treasury bills, notes and bonds are all referred to as *treasuries*. The difference in the designation is to distinguish between the length of maturity for each type instrument and how its interest is paid to you. Treasury bills have maturity dates up to 1 year. Treasury notes mature from 2 to 10 years from their issue date. Treasury bonds mature from 11 to 30 years from the date they were issued.

A unique form of U.S. Government Treasury is the zero coupon treasury. "Zero's" offer you safety, capital accumulation, assured rates of return, choice of maturities up to 30 years in the future, and excellent liquidity together with the full faith and credit of the U.S. Government. Zero's are purchased at a substantial discount to their face value. For example, a $1,000 "Zero" which matures 20 years in the future may be selling for 25% of its face value or, $250. This may provide you a yield of 7½% to maturity. When the bond matures you will receive a payoff from the Government of $1,000.

Government Agencies

Government Agencies usually stand alone from the financial strength of the government. Agencies can issue debt obligations independent of the U.S. Government treasury. They are rated AAA, the highest bond rating. Among the familiar reference to agencies may be Genny Mae's, Fannie Mae's, Freddy Mack's, and Sallie Mae's. Even though some of the references sound like they came from a college student's black book of dating acquaintances, they are acronyms for the initials of the separate agencies; For example: GNMA (Government National Mortgage Association), Genny Mae; FNMA (Federal National Mortgage Association, Fannie Mae; FHLMC (Farm Home Loan Mortgage Corporation), Freddie Mack;

SLMA (Student Loan Marketing Association), Sallie Mae. These agencies are corporations organized by the government to provide a market for banks and lending institution's to sell their mortgage and student loan portfolio's. GNMA is the only agency to carry the "full faith and credit" backing of the U. S. Government.

One consideration worth noting is the right of debtors to pay off their obligation at any time with no prepayment penalties. One might say, "good, I get my money back sooner." From a technical standpoint you are correct; however, although some people pay off their home mortgages because of moving or sale of their residence, others pay off their mortgage because interest rates have fallen and it is economical to refinance their home with a lower interest rate loan. If you have an investment in a GNMA that pays a yield of 12%, when the market rate of interest is 9%, you are happy, until you receive a pay-off (call) on your GNMA and you begin to look for a replacement investment. The disadvantage is not being able to lock in a fixed period of time for the favorable investment yield.

Collateralized Mortgage Obligations

Collateralized Mortgage Obligations (C.M.O.'s) are an investment in a pool of mortgages, most often on residential housing, in which you own a secured position. These are very similar to GNMA's and FNMA's, etc. You do not own any single mortgage, but you do own a proportionate amount of every mortgage in the pool. The mortgages are insured by an agency, usually of the Federal Government, consequently they are rated AAA and not subject to risk of loss of principle or accrued interest. The interest yield is usually consistent with the market interest for residential mortgages. Those whose homes are financed in the mortgage pool have the right to pay off their mortgage at any time without penalty. You may get a pay-off (call) of your position before you anticipate it. If you get a notice that you have been redeemed or called (received a pay off), the pay-offs are usually made in principle increments of $5,000 plus accrued interest. The same disadvantage of early pay-off exists with C.M.O.'s as with Government Agency issues.

Corporate Bonds

Corporate Bonds are debt obligations of corporations and usually carry a rating by one of the primary bond rating agencies, such as Moody's or Standard Poors. One of the primary advantages of corporate bonds is the predictable cash flow provided by a fixed rate of return. They usually pay a slightly higher rate of return than government securities.

The highest (best) rating is AAA. Ratings may also be as low as C. In some cases bonds are non-rated. Let's look at a bond rating scale.

AAA Highest rating. Capacity to pay interest and principle is extremely strong.

AA Strong capacity to repay interest and principle. Differs from the highest rating only in a small degree.

A Has strong capacity to repay interest and principle, although it is somewhat more susceptible to the adverse effects of changes in economic conditions.

BBB Adequate capacity to repay interest and principle. Adverse economic conditions are more likely to lead to a ·weakness in the capacity to pay interest and principle. Issues of this rating or higher are referred to as investment-grade bonds.

BB Predominately speculative bonds. Speculative by this reference is distinguished from investment grade. This is the highest of the speculative grades.

B More speculative than BB bonds. The likelihood of inability to pay interest and principle when due is somewhat higher.

CCC Higner degree of risk than the B ratings.

CC This is the highest degree of risk of any of the ratings. With this higher risk there may potentially be higher reward, as well as a higher likelihood of default.

C This rating is reserved for those bonds on which no interest is currently being paid.

NR Not rated by any rating agency. This may be the result of the issuing institution not applying for a rating. Bond rating agencies charge substantially for a complete review and the resultant rating. Bonds with this designation need to be evaluated independently of any rating service. They may or may not be good investment opportunities.

This is a scale similar to the one used by Standard Poors, a company which evaluates the credit worthiness and ability to meet financial obligations of bond issuing companies or municipalities. The scale used by Moody's varies somewhat. Moody's is another company that performs a comparable function of evaluation. Most bonds are rated by both institutions. The designated rating of a bond if it were the highest quality would appear like this; AAA/Aaa. AAA being the Standard Poors rating, and Aaa representing the opinion of Moody's. Occasionally you may see a + or − behind the alphabetic designation. This indicates a more finite breakdown within the rating.

Some issuing companies or municipalities also insure their bonds with companies that specialize in bond insurance. This insurance is a protection against default in the payment of interest and/or principle. Acceptable bond insurance by a reputable, recognized bond insurance company automatically gives bonds a AAA rating. However, all AAA-rated bonds are not necessarily insured. To protect your retirement dollars, you should look for high quality bonds, investment grade (BBB) or better. If you want to be ultra conservative, you should seek bonds that carry the AAA/Aaa rating, and possibly insurance. There are several insurance companies specializing in risk insurance for bonds. You may also find bonds are occasionally backed by irrevocable letters of credit (L.C.'s). In this event it would be necessary to evaluate the strength of the financial institution issuing the L.C. The insurance and/or L.C. is insurance against a default in the payment of principle and interest.

Interest on bonds is paid semi-annually. The interest on Corporate Bonds is subject to taxation by Federal, State and possibly Local Governments. Remember to take the tax obligation into account when figuring your "net" (spendable) yield.

Municipal Bonds

Municipal Bonds are debt obligations issued by local governments such as cities, towns, counties or states. Municipal bond ratings follow the same rating scale as corporate bonds. The primary difference from corporate bonds is that municipal bonds (Muni's) are free from taxation by the federal government and, in many states, free from taxation by the state government. Some states allow all "Muni's," an exemption from state tax. Other states may require the muni bond to be issued from within the state to receive state tax exemption. Your accountant or financial consultant in whom you have built the "doctor-type" trust, can guide you as to the tax treatment for your state. Don't overlook the power of earning interest that is free from taxation.

Muni bonds may be a general debt obligation of a municipality, referred to as a General Obligation Bond (G.O.). This means the issuing municipality has the authority to raise taxes to meet its obligation for the payment of principle and interest. Conversely, funds for the payment of principle and interest on a Revenue Bond are generated by revenue from the specific project for which the bond was issued. For example; a sewer improvement bond is a revenue bond that is retired by income from sewer assessments. Special purpose municipal bonds such as industrial development bonds, although referred to as "Muni's," may not be tax free. Be sure to check with your financial consultant on this important issue.

The following chart will be helpful as you evaluate your tax bracket, the yield on tax-free issues and the net spendable yield (*tax equivalent yield*) on tax-free issues. The chart assumes state tax exemption is available for the bond in question. All state taxes are figured at 7%

in addition to 15% and 28% federal tax brackets. In practice, Federal taxes are figured first then state tax is assessed on the residual income amount.

Taxable Equivalent Yields

Tax Free Interest Rate	15% fed + 7% state = 22%	28% fed + 7% state = 35%
5.0%	6.33%	7.46%
5.5%	6.96%	8.21%
6.0%	7.59%	8.96%
6.5%	8.22%	9.71%
7.0%	8.85%	10.45%
7.5%	9.48%	11.20%

Tax-deferred Annuities

Tax-deferred annuities are similar to C.D.'s except that they are issued by insurance companies. Remember the power of tax-deferred compounding? There are two kinds of tax defered annuities: *fixed* (those that bear a fixed interest rate like a C.D.), and *variable*. The variable annuity also allows tax deferral advantages however, the interest rate is not fixed or guaranteed. A variable annuity allows a variety of investment choices for your funds. It resembles a mutual fund, but it is tax deferred. Within the variable annuity you may elect to have, say . . . 30% of the money invested in a bond fund, 40% in a stock fund, and 30% in a money market fund. The selections you choose and the amount in each selection is "variable." Over an extended period of time, your variable annuity should increase to a higher value than its fixed-rate counterpart. However, you must be prepared for fluctuations in market value. Remember the discussion on asset allocation and diversification? Both types of annuities could have an appropriate place in a well diversified, conservative portfolio. The most important issue is your earnings grow tax deferred.

Annuities, whether fixed or variable, have other advantages also. Because they are issued by insurance companies and have a designated beneficiary, they have estate advantages. They pass to your estate or beneficiaries as if they were insurance. In other words, no necessity of probate.

Most annuities also have a liquidity feature allowing withdrawals each year. This amount may be the annual increase in value or 10% of the total value. A caution! If you are not 59½ years of age the withdrawal of your income may be subject to a 10% early withdrawal penalty tax imposed by the federal government. Annuity policies may also have a penalty for withdrawal in the early years after the contract is initiated. Regardless of which type annuity you choose, annuity payments received at retirement continue to be tax favored. This means when you receive a monthly, quarterly, semi-annual or annual annuity payment, part of each payment is a return of your capital therefore not subject to taxes.

Preferred Stock

Preferred Stock is an ownership position in the earnings of a corporation similar to common stock, except preferred stock has a prior claim on profits to pay dividends and unlike common stock, it usually does not have voting rights. You may have heard of a corporation reducing spending, suspending or eliminating its dividend. This usually refers to the dividend on common stock. Preferred dividends are usually cumulative, or they accumulate as a debt of the corporation even if they are not currently paid. They must be paid at some future date. Common dividends do not have this luxury status. If a common dividend is reduced, suspended or eliminated, the stock holder does not have any right to collect this lost income at a future date.

Preferred stock is usually categorized with bonds, in that it is like a fixed income investment, a corporate Board of Directors cannot eliminate the dividend as they can on a common stock, without having the preferred dividend being classified in default. The primary difference from a bond is bonds have a fixed maturity date, or a time in the future you will be paid back your principle by the company. Preferred stock may or may not have a maturity date (call date). If there is no call date on preferred stock, you must sell the stock to receive the return of your principle. If it has a call date, the company has the option to call in the stock and return the call value of the stock to you, (be careful on this one, before paying a premium over the call price be sure you understand the consquences).

Mutual Funds

Mutal Funds have gained great popularity over the past decades. For someone who does not want the obligation or headache of selecting specific investments to get proper diversification, a mutual fund may be a good choice. Mutual funds are pools of money gathered from investors, professionally managed and diversified into several investment choices. For example; an equity (stock) mutual fund may be established for the type stocks into which it invests. It may be a growth fund, one that buys companies having great growth potential for the future. These companies have sales, earnings and share of the market expanding faster than the general economy and their industry average; or, a value fund, one that invests in companies seemingly under priced compared to their perceived market value. Some mutual funds select only "blue chip" companies for their portfolio. Blue chip stocks are high-grade issues of major companies which have long and unbroken records of earnings and dividend payments. This term is used to describe the common stock of large, well established, stable, and mature companies of great financial strength. Some mutual funds may be structured as defensive funds. It has been said that "These consist of companies manufacturing goods that one eats, drinks, smokes or uses in the bathroom." The perception is that they are necessary goods or services which are "defensive" in a recessionary environment.

There are thousands of choices available for mutual fund selection. These include several different types of stock funds, bond funds, balanced funds (balanced between stocks and bonds or money market accounts), utility funds, international funds, and global funds, to name just a few. After meeting with your financial consultant, you will be able to select a mutual fund which meets your specific investment objectives. Mutual funds are sold by prospectus. The prospectus is published as a full disclosure of the investment management, disciplines, restrictions, and objectives. Take time to read it! It is published for your information and protection.

Professionally Managed Money

Professionally managed money has also been briefly addressed earlier in this chapter. It should be a consideration for anyone with $50,000 or more in his or her retirement account. The advantage of a professionally managed individual account over a mutual fund is, that managed-money portfolios are not pooled funds. In otherwords, the manager manages your personal portfolio without co-mingling your funds into a larger pooled portfolio. Your investment objectives are the only ones considered by the manager. You hire the manager to manage your investments and use his or her professional expertise to obtain the best performance within your established guidelines. When searching for a money manager, look for one that has expertise in managing funds within the investment guidelines and disciplines you establish, rather than finding a manager and expecting him to develop his expertise at your expense. This can be the very best choice for safety and performance.

Occasionally, a mutual fund may become so large managers may lose some of their effectiveness in managing the huge pool of assets while at the same time meeting the liquidity demands of investors who sell their mutual-fund holdings. The overall philosophy of whether to go it on your own, which admittedly some people do very effectively, or to hire a professional, is centered on the question, *can you manage the risk and still reap the rewards?*

Our old sage was born before they had eye tests and prescription glasses, so we're sure this isn't one of his sayings, but "Hind sight is always 20/20 vision." Over the years we have counseled with many people about retirement planning and budgeting and how to "make it happen." We, along with them, always have a very clear perspective of what should have happened and at what time of their lives it should have started. *Investing for retirement is fraught with perils if it is done through a rear view mirror.* Can you imagine what it would be like driving on a freeway, backwards, looking through the rear view mirror (and praying), hoping to herd the car to your destination without a major catastrophe?

Planning for first class retirement must be done through the front window, looking toward and planning for the future. The rear-view mirror is only intended to let you view the past. By the time you resort to looking in retrospect (rear view) that part of your actions or lack of planning is recorded in history, never to be changed. Plan for the future and discipline your life to make it happen! You are almost there!

8

Financial Peace Of Mind

The Seven Easy Steps

During a seminar on how to budget your money and prepare for retirement, a question was asked, "Can you give us some simple steps to follow to insure we are on the right track financially?" We noticed in the audience everyone was nodding their heads or looking to see what magic formula we would expound.

The answer to your question can be summed up in seven easy steps, we replied. We refer to these as the *Seven Easy Steps to Financial Peace of Mind.*

The first step is to live within your income. As we have discussed earlier, living within your income is the key to your current financial success as well as retiring first class. Once you manage your money, you'll be successful.

The *second step is to implement the Elephant Theory of Saving using the "percent-bite" method* as you live within your income. Remember if you can't save, you will become a financial slave.

Step three, *buy a home.* Sounds simple doesn't it? If you are managing your money properly, it is. The two greatest investments you will ever make are (1) investing time in the management of your money, and (2) buying your home.

The questions was asked, "What are the benefits of buying a home?" A hand was raised in the rear of the room, "Tax deductions."

We continued, What does it really mean, tax deductions? Did you know, you don't pay for 100% of your house payment? The government pays a portion of your mortgage payment each month. Let's say, for example, you pay $700 a month, of which $100 is principal and $600 is interest. Multiply $700 by 12 months, it equals $8,400. Of the $8,400, how much is interest?

A lady on the front row responded, "$600 times 12 equals $7,200."

Right you are. Your federal income tax-bracket is 15%. How much tax would you save by deducting the interest from your house payments?

A tall man stood with a calculator in hand and answered, "If $7,200 was the interest deducted and 15% is my tax bracket, I would multiply 15% times $7,200 of interest and get $1,080. Is that the taxes I would save?"

You're correct. In our illustration, you would save one thousand eighty dollars in federal income taxes. If your total house payments in one year equals $8,400, subtract your taxes saved of $1,080; the difference is $7,320. Divided by 12 months and the answer is $610. And . . . "

"Just a minute, you are moving too fast." Sorry, let's slow down a little. Let's have you review what we've discussed so far as you understand it.

"I'll be glad to. If I understand this right, my house payment is $700 a month, and you are trying to teach us what my actual out-of-pocket costs are when I deduct the interest and save taxes, right?"

You're correct and doing just great!

"All right, of my $700 monthly payment, $600 is my interest, and for one year my total interest paid is $7,200. I can deduct that from my income and reduce taxes—why everyone knows that. If my tax bracket is 15%, I multiply that by $7,200, and I get your answer of $1,080. But there is where I get lost."

Keep going, you're are doing great. Now figure out what your real out-of-pocket costs are on your house payment.

"If I'm saving $1,080 of actual tax dollars and . . . and . . . now I think I've got it! I would subtract the $1,080 from my total house payments per year of $8,400, and the difference would be my actual costs. Let's see $1,080 subtracted from $8,400 equals $7,320—divided by 12, equals $610. That means of my $700 a month house payment, I only pay $610, and the government pays $90."

Early Payoff of a Home Mortgage

Let's give this brave soul a great round of applause. Thank you very much for your help.

Another question was asked. "What's another good reason to buy a home?"

Someone in the class answered, "It is because I understand how to buy a home; wasn't that one of the rules?"

Yes, most people understand how to buy and sell a home for profit. Good.

"How about this question," said a couple about mid-way up the aisle. "If I mortgaged my home for thirty years and want to pay it off early, why shouldn't I use all my savings to pay off my mortgage?"

Excellent question. Remember the interest rule? "Them that understands it collects it, Them that don't pays it." The best methods, from our experience, to pay off your mortgage early are the following which do not deplete your savings.

Our first suggestion is to make double principal payments on your outstanding mortgage each month. Since the smallest amount of your monthly mortgage payment is your principal portion to make two of these each month should be easy for you.

In order to make the correct payment amount, you should call your mortgage company to verify you can make double principal payments on your loan. Most mortgage companies will agree to this procedure unless your mortgage agreement doesn't permit you to prepay any or all of your principal.

Next, find your copy of your mortgage amortization schedule. If you don't have the original amortization schedule of your mortgage, just ask your mortgage company for one. They will be happy to send you a duplicate. You will need this document to assist you in keeping tract of the double principal payments paid.

As you look at this document, whatever the principal amounts of your house payment are, make two of those per month until you feel the payments are getting too large and will no longer fit into your budget.

To illustrate, let's say your mortgage is $100,000 at 10% interest for 30 years. The principal and interest is $878 per month. Your mortgage company will permit you to make double principal payments each month.

In our illustration, we will only use the first six payments of our amortization schedule as the example. Our first six mortgage payments with principle and interest are as follows:

Payment	Total	Principal	Interest
1	$878	$45.00	$833.00
2	$878	$46.00	$832.00
3	$878	$47.00	$831.00
4	$878	$52.00	$826.00
5	$878	$57.00	$821.00
6	$878	$63.00	$815.00

If you wanted to make double principal payments, your first total house payment is the following:

First principal payment:	$ 45.00
Second principal payment:	$ 46.00
First interest payment:	$833.00
Total amount of the 1st house payment:	$924.00

The second total house payment, while doubling principal payments, is the following:

Third principal payment:	$ 47.00
Fourth principal payment:	$ 52.00
Second interest payment:	$832.00
Total amount of the 2nd house payment:	$931.00

The third total house payment in our example of paying double principal payments, is the following:

Fifth principal payment:	$ 57.00
Sixth principal payment:	$ 63.00
Third interest payment:	$831.00
Total amount of the 3rd house payment:	$951.00

If you continued to make double principal payments for your entire mortgage term, your mortgage would be paid in half the time. Note how your principal payments are increasing as each payment is paid. Since the mortgage company is permitting you to make these additional principal payments, they will make the actual principal and interest adjustments on the mortgage loan for you. At year end you should receive a statement reflecting these additional principal payments on the mortgage.

There may come a time in your double-principal-payment schedule when your ability to continue doubling principal payments will have to terminate. However, you should make them as long as you can. Remember, your house payment increased from $878 to $924, to $931, and $951, in our example, due to increasing your principal payments.

Here's another idea to pay your mortgage off faster. Whenever you get your tax refund, make an extra house payment with it and apply it to your principal. When you make this a habit, this tradition will shorten your mortgage length.

Another idea to reduce your mortgage is to set aside a certain amount each year equal to one or two house payments from your savings. Apply these amounts to the principal as well.

As a final suggestion, you may want to have a combination of all three methods. Living within your income will assist you in paying off your mortgage earlier rather than using all of your savings.

Everyone seemed to understand, They were commenting to themselves, "First thing Monday morning I'll call the mortgage company to see if I can make double principal payments . . . and will that help me pay my loan off sooner? By how many years? Check the budget to make sure we can make those extra principal payments.

The big number four, is *investing in your IRA*. The greatest advantage of an IRA is tax deferral until retirement. This tax deferral process helps your retirement nest egg grow at a much faster rate. Use the George Thomas Financial Rule to help you calculate your retirement goal along the way.

Accumulate a Year's Supply

Number five is *using the Elephant Theory of Savings* to help you accumulate a year's supply of money.

"Yeah. Sure. A year's supply of money? You're not serious are you," were the replies.

We are very serious. Why can't you save a year supply of money?

"Not in one year, we couldn't, someone retorted in the rear of the room.

If you saved 10% of your gross income every year for ten years, how much income would you have prudently saved?

"A years supply," a couple shouted.

You're right. Even if it took you 5, 10, or 15 years to accomplish it, you would have succeeded where very few have.

"How much is a year's supply of money?" came the question.

"Wouldn't it be my gross income for one year?," another person asked.

Good Question. It should be what you need to meet expenses for one year, not one year's income.

Do you feel it's prudent to have a year's supply of food, clothing, and fuel for emergencies? Why not a years supply of money to make it complete. By using the Elephant Theory of Savings with the "percent bite" method, you can achieve this most worthy financial goal.

As we counsel people about their financial emergencies, they usually get very concerned about any sudden financial drain. And rightly so. But if you think four new tires on the car is a real emergency, how about a spouse being out of work for a prolonged period of time?

Or what about six months of disability without medical coverage? The number one concern is unemployment for any period of time. As you can see a year's supply of money would help relieve these financial worries. A financial emergency has been defined as *"too much month at the end of the money.'"*

You need to start your year's supply of money now to help compensate for the partial or total loss of your financial exposure. Remember, an ounce of financial prevention is worth a ton of borrowed money in a financial emergency.

Reduce Your Debt-Payment Percentage

Number six, *monitor and reduce your debt payment percentage until it is 0%*. What is your debt payment percentage? It is your current monthly debt payments as compared to your gross monthly income.

An example, let's say you make $2,000 per month. Your debt payments total $900. To calculate your debt payment percentage, divide your total debt payment per month ($900) by your total gross income per month ($2,000). Your debt payment percentage is ($900 divided by $2,000) 45%. This means 45% of your gross monthly income is being paid out to someone else for debt!

Do you remember the interest rule? "Them that understands it collects it; Them that don't pays it." At a 45% debt payment percentage, you are at the opposite end of the interest rule from where you want to be.

We suggest your debt payment percentage be zero. We feel debt should only be incurred for two reasons: (1) the purchase of a home, and (2) the purchase of an education. The purchase of a home we have already discussed in number three. The purchase of an education is an investment in your future earning potential.

We can hear your questions, "But I have already incurred debt; what debt payment percentage should I aim for until I can whittle it down to zero?"

The answer is 35%. *Your debt payment percentage should never exceed 35% of your gross monthly income for all your current debt.* Current debt would include your house payment, credit cards, personal debt, and relative debt (money borrowed from relatives), etc. As you live within your income and save, you may want to have a specific budget category titled debt reduction to start getting your debt reduced to a 0%.

Let's quickly illustrate how a 0% debt payment percentage can quickly increase your spendable monthly income without any more work! In our example, you have a 35% debt payment percentage plus a tax bracket of 20% for all taxes due, for a total of 55%. Net spendable income after debt and taxes would be 45% (100% total monthly income minus 55% debt payment percentage and Taxes equals 45% left to spend). This 45% represents what you now have to live on until the next pay period.

Consider this: if your debt payment percentage was 0%, your total taxes 20%, your net spendable income would be a wonderful 80% (100% minus 20% equals 80%) not 45%. With the budget and savings tips contained in this book, over time you should be able to reduce your debt payment percentage to 0%!

The last step, number seven, *build your retirement now,* can be summed up on a sign we once read on an office calculator which stated, *Do it!, do it right!, do it right now.*

Think about your retirement right now. Use the financial instruments you have been taught in this book, and you will get excellent investment results.

Then, picture the quality of life you desire for your retirement. Remember, what the mind sees and believes, it will achieve. See it and believe it. Prepare now and it will happen.

There is an old saying which states, *If you are prepared you need not fear.* Or as we say, If you're prepared, you won't be scared. Preparation is the key to success, regardless of your age."

These seven steps to Financial Peace of Mind will secure your financial future, and thanks for coming.

As the people exited, they felt they could live within their income, save money, buy a home or improve it, contribute to an IRA, get started on a years supply of food, clothing, fuel, and money, get their debt payment percentage to 0%, and prepare for retirement now.

In the next chapter, you will learn how to shift your financial gears into a great retirement. So let's turn the page and continue to build your retirement.

9

The Great Gear Change

The powerful diesel tractor, trailed by the lengthy van loaded with its 40,000 pound payload, sped over the freeway toward the mountain-pass. Marve, a skilled driver trained in the ability to bring together the power of the engine, the strength of the transmission, and the balance of the load, looked forward to the challenge of the mountain. His knowledge, training, and skill of execution, coupled with the power of the truck, moved the production of the country to the waiting markets of the world.

Starting up the mountain pass the truck traveled with great speed and momentum. But as the truck ascended the mountain, the earth's powerful gravitational pull tugging at the heavy load rapidiy slowed the truck, requiring a change of gears.

The gear change is much more complex than just moving the shift lever to a different position. The gear shift lever is small, but it controls great power. Marve checked the tachometer for the engine speed which must be synchronized with the gears and vehicle movement. His training and skill allowed him to ease the gears into the next range at precisely the right moment when the engine and transmission meshed without effort. If he missed that moment, it would require acceleration of the motor and double clutching to complete the change without damaging the power train of the vehicle.

The matching of power and speed would be adjusted several times before reaching the summit. At the summit Marve joined several other truckers checking their loads, tires, and the condition of their rig, before continuing on their journey.

The need to change gears typifies the experience of shifting into retirement. Depending on your speed, the slope of the mountain

ahead, the length of the climb, and your preparation and implementation, you can experience a flawless transition and enjoy your journey
to the summit of change—your retirement.

All too often, when it's time to change financial and activity gears,
or retire, the speed of the engine driving your activity motors is not
synchronized with your financial gears, and thus is not ready for
the change.

The Second Sixty Days

A friend of ours tells the story of his happily married neighbors
who, after working extremely hard their entire lives, finally arrived
at those long awaited, golden years of retirement. The first 60 days
went by beautifully. All those little "honey-do's" that had accumulated
over the years were now "honey done's," and it was now time for
togetherness. Ah yes, togetherness!

After a time, it seemed the coveted association they dreamed of
for so long was getting a little less dreamy, and the blissful couple
felt their closeness needed a little distance.

Have you ever had one of those days when everything said was
taken wrong? It had been one of those days. She finally exclaimed,
"This is enough!" She went to the front of the house where she could
feel sorry for herself in private. "Imagine! after all these years,
discovering I have married an uncaring clod, and I call him my
husband."

Not to be outdone by her attitude of needing some space, he retired
to his only real pastime in life: the loveable, understanding television
set, with its Saturday Sports Spectacular. It was in a humble little
spot at the back of the house, somewhat out of the way, but he thrived
in his own little kingdom. "The TV, my chair, and that incredible
monarch of the wilderness a six-point buck. What a hunt it was; and
to think she called it a 'stupid dust catcher.'"

The intensity of the day built to the danger level. Conflict rather
than compatibility lurked at every doorway. She knew she needed
help just to survive without blowing a gasket.

"I need my medication for relaxing and forgetting the world. One might help, but two surely will."

After a half hour with no results, she decided she needed one more dose for relaxation.

Then the comedy really lurched forward. The pills began taking effect. The dizzy feeling, slightly blurred vision, slowed thought process, and slurred speech which all seemed to be saying, "relax, go to sleep," were interrupted by a remnant of her fading consciousness.

"I'm in trouble and this is getting real scary!"

She needed real help, now! All this had taken place without the slightest knowledge of her unsympathetic companion who was totally involved in the third down and long yardage.

Who did she call for help? Not the loving companion of forty-five years. "I'll show him," she thought. as she struggled with the phone. The dial appeared fuzzy. "Isn't that cute? A fuzzy wuzzy phone dial. I've never seen one like that before. Let's see 991. No! Oh yea, its 91111. That ought to get the 'Marapedics' here in a hurry."

The sheriff, paramedics, and the ambulance all arrived within minutes of her call. Red lights, blaring radio and all the other commotion that goes with an emergency, including concerned and inquisitive neighbors, unfolded in their front yard.

The paramedics entered the door, assisted her onto the stretcher, checked her vital signs, then wheeled her to the waiting ambulance. About this time the unconcerned husband, part-time sports buff, noticed a little stir on his own ten yard line. Ignoring the fact that on his stroll through their small but adequate home he had not seen his wife, he leisurely wandered out the front door. With thumbs locked behind his suspenders, he stepped into the yard only to be greeted by the anxious squadron of emergency vehicles, flashing lights, and concerned onlookers.

Without breaking his leisurely pace, he sauntered up to the side of the stretcher upon which his loving wife and companion lay peacefully still. The pale color of her skin and the forced smile on her face were the obvious result of a mild overdose. The busy paramedics were covering her with a modesty sheet in preparation for her trip to the hospital emergency room.

Carefully surveying the situation, as only a husband who has had his football game interrupted can do, he snorted, "Where the h____ do you think you're going?"

An armchair philosopher once stated, "Retiring is one thing; but, being retired is a whole different experience." This couple began to realize it upon returning from the hospital.

Being retired, the different experience, has as many excitements as one would want to encounter in a lifetime. It has been likened to adjusting to marriage all over again. Another seasoned companion expressed, "There's good news and bad news about Fred being retired. The good news is, Fred is going to be around the house a little more. The bad news is, Fred is going to be around the house a little more." Too many husbands think since they are retired, life is just fun and games for evermore. A husband may overlook the fact that for his companion, the activity schedule hasn't changed. She has all her former assignments as well as coping with another meddler in her workshop area, the kitchen. The Immortal Sage speaks again, "A man who says he is the boss in his home (referring to the workshop area of his wife) will lie about other things also."

More Than Just Money

We have discussed many aspects of retiring first class, most of which have been centered around budgeting and financial security. There is another issue equally important. Even if you are the most financially secure person in the world, regardless of whether you are single or married, you need a purpose in life. Developing this purpose is an art. We find the happiest people in the world are the busiest, and the most involved—those with a purpose.

A friend of ours related his experience with an elderly couple seated on the front porch of their homey little abode. "Recently, they began to spend more hours in their rocking chairs. The chairs creaked rhythmicaliy as they rocked in the afternoon sun. He, being overcome with a tinge of nostalgia, looked over at his sweetheart of many years, patted her on the knee and said, 'I'm surely proud of you.' She looked with admiration at him, and although she was a little hard of hearing she knew precisely what he had said. This opportunity for a moment of fun was too great for her to pass up. She smiled as she replied, 'Yes dear, I'm a little tired of you too.'"

There can be great loneliness in togetherness. Those who have not developed tact, tolerance, patience, and a great deal of love, may find when the change is made to retirement mode, they feel as if they are alone on an isolated island, having no one to share feelings and expressions with. Hopefully those who have companions are ready for the change. Remember the couple who was enjoying too much togetherness? People-time is important, and must be quality, enjoyable, sharing time—a time for expressing feelings and listening to expressions.

Our wise Sage stated, "The Lord gave us two ears and one mouth for a purpose. We're supposed to listen twice as much as we talk."

Without proper planning, single folks may also find retirement a very lonely time of their life. You have previously had people time, at work on a daily basis. Your original thoughts of retirement seemed exciting. Now you must find new activities and support groups to share this newly created time. These activities may fill the void created by the lack of personal relationships previously experienced on the job.

Develop An Activity Plan

What is the solution? If retiring is viewed as a gear change rather than a complete restructuring of the system, the transition can be fun and very exciting. Starting early, and planning for your new schedule will allow you to accomplish all your dreams.

Like planning for the financial aspects of retiring first class, the social and emotional areas require pre-planning also. To retire without an activity plan is certain to put stress on this part of your life. Here are a few ideas.

Personal Development Through Education

Reading. Writing. Take classes at the local university or community education facility (It isn't too late to graduate). *Take music lessons. Take a computer class.*

Hobbies

Knitting. Crochet the afghan you have always wanted. Woodworking. Wood Carving. Painting. Start a fix-it shop or home craft shop. Bake cookies for the neighborhood. Restore antiques. Build models. Ceramics. Collect Dolls.

Service:

Visit neighbors, relatives or your children (Remember the old adage? Get revenge, live long enough to be a problem to your kids). *Do service work at a local hospital. Volunteer at a local school. Work at the local center for handicapped. Volunteer at the senior citizens' center. Volunteer for service to a local Boy Scout, Cub Scout, or Girl Scout group* (It will keep you young, and add a new dimension to your life as well as the lives of the young people with whom you work and share experience). *Be active in your church* (—your Minister, Bishop, Priest or Rabbi will love you for it). *Perform musical selections at a local rest home.*

Sports

Golf (A client told us of Jim, a senior citizen golfer friend of his who began to lose his eyesight but didn't want to give up the game. The eye doctor suggested he find a golfing buddy that had good eyesight who could accompany him and watch the ball. The partner was found. Bill tolerated the extensive inquiry about his eyesight. Convinced this was the answer, Jim arranged for the first of the "twosome tournaments." Jim teed up the ball and inquired of Bill, "Are you ready? Now be sure to watch it!"

"O.K."

Jim hit a beautiful drive, long and straight, right down the middle of the fairway. He turned to Bill and said,

"Did you see it?"

"Yup, I saw it."

After walking some distance down the fairway Jim said to Bill, "Now, you saw the ball?"

" Yup."

"Where'd it go?"

Bill haltingly replied, "I can't remember."

Swimming. Bowling. Walking. Jogging. Biking. Horse shoes. Skeet shooting. Join a sports facility. Hand ball. Racquet ball. Tennis. Riding horses. Enjoy nature. Hunt. Fish. (Have you seen the bumper sticker which states, "Time spent fishing cannot be deducted from a man's life?")

Travel

Travel to the place you have always dreamed of and budgeted for. Join a travel club. Affiliate with a local university travel club (They travel to the most scenic and exotic spots on the globe by film and with a live narration). *Spend time touring your city* (it might surprise you what beauties are in your own back yard).

It may sound like we are appealing only to those who choose to retire at 65. We really refer to anyone preparing to experience the "great gear change," whether you are age 30 or 80-plus. Retiring isn't by any means the end of the line; it is the beginning of a new adventure with a different set of gears and a different speed, regardless of age.

Colonel Sanders, the originator of Kentucky Fried Chicken, appeared as a guest on a talk show. At the time, he was in his late eighties. The host of the show asked, "Why do you still work every day? You obviously have enough money to retire and not worry about anything for the rest of your life." The Colonel replied, "Money? Retire? Worry? Hummmmmm. Those are interesting thoughts." He continued, "When I was much younger, someone drove an old car out to the farm and abandoned it there, not too far from the barn.

It wasn't in too bad of shape. It sat there for about two years. After a time there wasn't much left of it. It had just rusted away. I kind'a figure a fella' is about the same. He'll probably rust out long before he wears out."

John D. Rockefeller made a million dollars a week while in his mid-50's. As you might suspect, this type activity comes with its own degree of built in-stress. Concerned family and friends encouraged him to see his doctor for a physical exam. The doctor gave some life-prolonging advice in a capsule of four easy rules:

1. Push away from the table while you are still hungry.
2. Get some physical exercise every day.
3. Stop worrying.
4. Eliminate stress.

Mr. Rockefeller died after 90-plus productive years.

The Retired Sage once claimed, "Just when I get all the answers figured out, nobody asks the questions anymore."

Many Begin Productive Undertakings After Retirement

Quite unlike this feeling, we are reminded of historical events that exemplify the ability of experienced individuals to continue their works and accomplishments throughout their mature years; not for personal gain or recognition, but for the benefit of generations yet to come.

Many notable people throughout history started their most productive undertakings at an age when many others would think of retiring as a stopping point, not a new beginning.

At the age of 71, Golda Meir became Prime Minister of Israel and served for five years.

At the age of 77, John XXIII was elected Pope and brought a new perspective to administration in the Catholic Church.

At the age of 80, Voltaire led France's struggle for greater respect for the rights of mankind.

At age 81, Benjamin Franklin traveled to the Constitutional Convention to add his wisdom to the drafting of the inspired document that has become the model of democracy for the world. Franklin is the only one of the founding fathers to have signed all four of the significant documents establishing the freedom of this union: The Declaration of Independence, Treaty of Alliance with France, Treaty of Peace with Great Britain, and the Constitution of the United States Of America.

His last act of public service was to sign an appeal to congress calling for the speedy abolition of slavery. The fruits of this effort became a reality nearly 100 years later.

He died in 1790 at the age of 84. Nearly 20,000 people attended his memorial services. His name is revered to this day.

At age 83, Barbara McClintock won the Nobel Prize for researching genetics.

At age 89, Frank Lloyd Wright completed the famous Gugenheim Museum.

After passing the age of 500, Noah began construction on the Ark which, when he was 600 years old, ascended the great flood and preserved mankind and the animal kingdom on the earth.

Develop The Prize Within You

A principle of self worth is to develop the prize within you. Your past experience is the prize. No one can duplicate it; only you can share it. You have so much to give, especially in years when the pressure of financial gain lessens, and you are enjoying the benefits of your diligent budgeting for successful retirement. Your new time schedule allows for more diversified activities.

The nation is beginning to realize what a prize the "experienced" community is. Those who have a little more time, because of retirement, are now sought after to give counseling, assist in managing businesses, direct great works of service, and occupy part-time jobs. Businesses are increasingly aware that retired or semi-retired people are a great asset to their establishments. "They're happy, they like to associate with our customers, they know what they are talking about, people like to be assisted by them, and they're dependable," a business and community leader commented. "They are really looking for some way to serve and to assist the community with their valuable experience. For the most part they are not looking to build monuments, they are interested in the public welfare. They are needed and appreciated."

Tycho Brahe had worked most of his life to perfect a system of tracking the stars in the heavens. He also refuted the 2,000-year-old Copernicus Theory of the revolution of the stars. He knew there had to be a logical method of mapping the heavens and naming stars for future generations.

He was advancing in years, and if his work was to continue for future generations, he must find someone to whom he could teach his system and share his discoveries. He prayed incessantly for inspiration on finding this special person. Responding to a knock at his door, he was confronted by a young man who introduced himself as Johannes Kepler. Kepler had studied astronomy and was aware of Brahe's work. He sought him out to learn more about his discoveries.

Many weeks were spent instructing Kepler on mapping the heavens, and the errors in the ancient Copernicus Theory. His system allowed for the identification of hundreds of stars. Time moved on and Kepler could see the health of Brahe begin to deteriorate. He encouraged Brahe to publish his work so proper credit could be given to him for his miraculous discoveries.

Tycho Brahe exemplified the principles of dedication and service. He did not want personal credit for his work, nor did he want his name immortalized; he wanted Kepler to pursue the work to its completion for the benefit of mankind. The credit could go to Kepler. Brahe's satisfaction was in knowing it would be done.

When Kepler insisted the credit go to the original founder of the system. Brahe said, "*Many discover and pursue for personal gain.*

To them go the palms, the shouting, and the praise; ours be the father's glory in the son." Johannes Kepler was humbled by Brahe's attitude. The system developed by Tycho Brahe and the subsequent discoveries of Johannes Kepler regarding the elliptical orbit of planets have opened scientific doors to countless additional astronomical discoveries. May the palms and the praise be theirs forever.

A more current example of this concern for the benefit of mankind are the words of Neil Armstrong as he stepped on to the surface of the moon; the first man to be so honored.

"One small step for man. One giant leap for mankind."

Long ago a noble and wise king delivered a powerful message to his people. His spirit abounded with love and understanding for the importance of each person in the kingdom.

"I, whom you call your king, am no better than you are . . . .

"I have labored with my own hands to save you taxes; not that I might boast, but that I can answer you with a clear conscience."

He went on counseling them to avoid conflicts at all costs, to love and serve one another. He continued, "When you are in the service of your fellow beings, you are only in the service of your God."

Evan and Myrtle

Evan and Myrtle have developed their special talent of love and service over many years. It has been the basis for a most interesting and rewarding retirement. Public service is no stranger to them. They have also been actively involved in their religion their entire lives. All the principles we have discussed about preparing for first class retirement have been personified by this lovely couple. Through our relationship with them we have become well acquainted with their formula for success. We share this phenomenal story with you.

In Myrtle's words, "We're not wealthy, but we live comfortably. We have always been able to live on our income. During the Great Depression there were times when the next meal may have been in question, but we always seemed to get by."

Their frugal nature and their willingness to work proved to be their salvation during the depression. Evan took a job with the government, teaching boys, most coming from the Eastern States, how to work. They built fences across miles of forest land, and fire-watch towers to aid in forestry fire control. Myrtle stayed home at the ranch, tended the animals and raised the children while caring for the field and row crops. The crops didn't do well that year because of the drought. This compounded their problems because the seed was now gone and there was no money to buy more for next year. A woman ranching alone wasn't a fun experience, although it has been the source of much laughter when viewed in retrospect. Building fences and forest structures wasn't much fun either, especially with a group of young men who had never had to work and didn't know the difference between a hammer and a shovel. This too is now looked upon with humor and smiles. They realize, *minor tragedy* + *time* = *humor.*

Hoping to find more stable employment. and having survived the depression, Evan and Myrtle decided to move back to the city. A job was found in the construction industry. Construction in those days was a fair job but certainly not a place to get rich. Each payday, no matter how small the pay proceeds for the week, 10% of the paycheck went into a savings account.

"Most of the investment choices we have today were unknown then. The passbook savings account was the choice for most people. Interest was about 3%. For the most part, our retirement savings were invested in the safety of insured savings, balanced occasionally with some utility stocks, and more recently in a conservative mutual fund," Evan modestly remarked.

Their savings have provided security and adequate growth for a substantial retirement account. In addition. They have the benefit of their monthly Social Security check. Budgeting is a wonderful habit with them. They still save monthly, including 10% of their Social Security. Budgeting, no debt, and saving have become a part of their life style.

We define "life style" as something which has become common-place. It is done so routinely it's natural, yet, viewed as a necessity. For some people this may mean high living and spending. For Myrtle and Evan, it is service and saving. As we inquired about their lifestyle, they looked at us quisically whenever we mentioned service and saving. They couldn't understand what was so unique about routine items that "one just does."

They have always had the money to do whatever they want because they budgeted for all of their hopes, desires, and dreams.

"Our life style hasn't changed after retirement. We just keep on doing what we have always done. I'm not sure we've even slowed down. We have time to do what we enjoy most. We just do more of it. The real wealth we enjoy is our family and our dear friends, Myrtle observed.

Little folks from the neighborhood, and some not so little folks, affectionately call them "Grandma and Grandpa," even though there is no blood relationship. The little folks know "Grandma" is always good for a cookie. "All they have to do is ring the doorbell and look hungry," she laughed with a twinkle in her eye.

Rarely does an evening go by that someone isn't dropping in just to say hello. Grandchildren and great grandchildren frequently visit and totaly enjoy playing games with their Grandparents. It's about a stand off, determining who has the most fun. Idle conversation such as "Let's go get some ice cream," is taken very seriously. Before the sentence is finished, they have their coats and are ready to go.

The spark of youth has never gone dim in their hearts. They reminisce occasionally when asked about the "olden days," but most often they enjoy hearing about current activities of family and friends especialiy the young people.

They have worked together making quilts for all 23 of their grandchildren. They read, cook, bake, and quilt together. They have an ongoing friendly banter about how to interpret certain recipes from the kitchen. Speaking of the kitchen, Myrtle elaborated. "Oh, he finally gets to the end result. He just takes the long way around

to get there. I just close my eyes to the mess and let him have at it."
They both laughed at the comment. They exemplify a significant
principle of human relationships. Differences of opinion are healthy,
not a source of conflict. We are sure this is also a sign of a very mature
and loving relationship.

Evan has become proficient in wood carving; they have both done
some painting. Their works of art are surprisingly good for not having
started until long after most of us would have thought it too late to
learn.

Evan's pride and joy is his garden, which supplies most of his
children, many of his grandchildren, and a portion of the neighborhood with fresh produce in the summer and fruits in the fall.

Evan was having a problem with a gopher eating off the roots in
his prized garden. He tried everything from running the waterhose
in the gopher hole, in hopes of drowning the varmit, to car exhaust
fumes and poisoned peanuts. Nothing worked. The unconquerable
gopher mounds still appeared every morning. After surveying the
water damage in their basement caused by the attempted drowning
of the gopher. Evan decided to get serious about this furry intruder.
Over the smiling protests of Mytle, Evan avowed, "This requires
some drastic action." Removing his prized weapon from its storage
case, he loaded up the 12-gauge shotgun and took his battle position
on the back porch. Having been raised on a farm, early mornings
and shotguns were not strangers to him. Soon after daybreak the
industrious rodent routinely appeared, burrowing around the garden
enjoying his morning meal. This day Mr. Gopher made a serious
mistake. He decided to venture into the unexplored greenhouse. On
to the stoop in front of the greenhouse door he cautiously crept. "That
glorified rat! He's heading into my greenhouse," fumed Evan.
KaBooooom!!!!! bye-bye gopher. Oh, Oh! Problem. Evan had just
blown a hole in the corner of his greenhouse. Yes, the spark of youth
is still there. They both laughed as Evan related this comical incident,
and Myrtle joked, "You can take the boy off the farm, but you can't
take the farm out of the boy."

At their home, there is always a soft shoulder and a listening ear, a warm heart and a smile, the smell of home-made bread, happiness, and the true life example of retiring first class. The dream of their early married life has come true: "be financially secure, stay active, and spend our lives serving others!" stated Evan.

The art of retiring first class is developed by planning and then by doing. Those who enjoy the greatest and earliest success are the ones who implement the plan. Many people may spend a lifetime planning. Some of those plans would make the professional planner look weak. Unfortunately, the best plan in the world is worthless unless it is put into practice. As the architect proclaimed, "People can't live in a plan. It is the implementation of the plan, completion of construction, and use of the facility that provides enjoyment and security."

Financial security is a most important ingredient of a successful retirement plan. However, implementing your plan for social and emotional change is also a key to happiness and the culmination of your lifetime of preparation. Plan now and implement your plan. Learning to enjoy other people's success and sharing your talents with them will greatly enhance your ability to become what you want to be.

Now let's learn the Financial Power Formula.

10

The Financial Power Formula

Everyday in some periodical or television commercial, and in everyday business lingo the word *power* is mentioned. One television commercial stressed the all-important power lunch. Another emphasized the power positions of the world. *Power, power, power,—* the call of those seeking financial success. In this chapter you are going to learn about the greatest influencing power—*financial power,* and most important: *your* financial power.

Remember the Golden Rule? We mean the financial Golden Rule. The rule is, *He who has the gold makes the rules.* In discussing your retirement, you have the gold everyone seeks; you make the rules.

As you prepare for retirement or actually retire, the gold seekers will be after your pot of retirement gold. Since you have the gold, you can make the rules, and they will be obedient to your every wish and command.

To protect your golden nest egg from gold seekers, inflation, financial reversals, and the proclaimed "perfect" investment, here is a financial formula for you to determine a potentialy successful investment for your retirement dollars.

The financial formula which will keep your retirement investments golden is made up of the word POWER. Each letter of the word POWER means a key ingredient of this successful financial formula.

P = Principal Safe

Is the investment you're considering protecting your accumulated principal against most or all financial hazards? Remember what we have related to you in this book: it is better for you to get a return *of* your principle rather than *on* your principle. If you don't have investment or principle, you don't have anything. The protection of your investment principle is the first consideration of your retirement investment.

O = Optimum Cash Flow

Does the investment you're considering have the optimum cash flow you need to have a great retirement? Will it produce a golden stream of income for you when you need it? Can you receive these golden offsprings monthly, quarterly, semiannually, or annually? How often do you need the income to continue the life-style to which you have become accustomed? Can this retirement investment produce your income stream need? Will these golden distributions reduce your hard-saved financial principle?

W = Wealth Preserver

How many years will it or did it take you to accumulate your retirement nest egg? Is the investment you are considering preserving your wealth by giving you an adequate investment return to protect your golden stream of income against inflation? Will it protect your purchasing power? Will it give you now or in the future, principle-erosion protection?

E = Easily Understood

Is the investment to which you will be committing your hard-earned money easily understood by you? Recently a television commercial stated, "If you don't understand it, we won't let you buy it." Let's put it another way—if you don't understand it, *don't even consider it without sound advice from your financial consultant!* Only invest in financial instruments or investments you understand. Financial ignorance breeds poverty rather quickly, so be careful.

Financial common sense will tell you, "If you don't understand it, don't do it," before you are counseled by your trusted financial consultant.

R = Risk/return Percentage

The risk/return percentage theory states if you are trying to obtain more than a 16% annual return on your retirement funds, you must be willing to accept a greater degree of investment or market risk. Forget all the charts, graphs, computer printouts, barkers, and other financial promises. Just remember the risk/return percentage. If you want more than 16%, get ready to take upon yourself, ulcer-rated market risk or even financial loss! We have quoted an old investment adage which states, "If it sounds too good to be true, it usually is!"

Now you understand what the word POWER represents. Let's discuss how to use it so you can invest in safe, stable, secure investments which should give you a successful investment for your retirement funds.

The Power Point System

Each letter of the word POWER, as you now know, represents an investment ingredient which will assist you in choosing a good investment for your retirement nest egg. To use this successful financial formula, we assign each letter of the word POWER a point system. Each letter represents five POWER points. If the investment is superior in all aspects, it would receive twenty-five points, five points for each letter of the word POWER. If the investment under consideration receives twenty-five POWER points, it is worth your time and consideration for further due diligence or financial investigation and possible investment. Remember the "perfect" investment has five points for each letter of the word POWER or a total of 25 points. This "perfect" 25 points will assist you in making the proper investment decision by helping you chose the "perfect" investment for your retirement.

Let's use an example to illustrate how to use it. You are considering investing in the real estate market. Knowing the PCWER formula, you get out a piece of paper and a pencil. On the left-hand side of the paper, you write the word POWER down the margin of the sheet. Next to each letter of the word POWER, you write 1-2-3-4-5, representing the total points available for each letter of the POWER formula (see figure 1).

Figure 1

P   1-2-3-4-5
O   1-2-3-4-5
W   1-2-3-4-5
E   1-2-3-4-5
R   1-2-3-4-5

You are ready to analyze your current investment opportunity. To evaluate the investment properly, ask yourself these questions and answer them by giving your "financial feelings" a numerical value from 1-5 points. Here are some questions you may ask and how you may score it.

Investment: Real Estate

1. P-(*principle safe?*) Is this investment going to be principle safe? Probably not. Is it going to keep my hard-earned principle intact at all times? Not all the time. Can I get at my principle if I need it? If I have the time to sell it. I'll give it 3 POWER points."

2. O-(*optimum cash flow?*) Will this investment produce the quarterly income I need to add to my current retirement income? No. I'll give it 0 POWER points.

3. W-(*wealth preserver?*) Will this investment preserve my purchasing power? Probably not—real estate values have been declining in my area. Will it hedge against inflation since it is fully paid for? Even though property values are down, it is growing faster than inflation. I'll give it 3 POWER points.

4 E-(*easily understood?*) Do I understand buying real estate? yes. Do I fully understand the buying and potential sale of this piece of property? Yes. I'll give it 5 points."

5 R-(*risk/return percentage?*) Is this investment making more than 15%? No. Then the risk should be OK. I'll give it 4 points.

Once you have graded your investment feelings and converted your feelings into POWER points, you need to change your POWER points into the *investment success percentage.* The investment success percentage indicates your investment probability for success represented in a percentage. Here's how we suggest you use it.

6. *investment success percentage calculation:* Add up the POWER points: $3 + 0 + 3 + 5 + 4$ equals 15 POWER points. To convert your POWER points into an investment success percentage, You divide 15 by 25. (Remember from our earlier discussion, 25 points is the "perfect" investment. By using 25 points as the divisor, it will give you a more accurate feeling as to the probability of success of your investment, currently under consideration, as measured by the "perfect" investment.) Fifteen divided by 25 is 60%. The 60% tells you that you have a 60% chance of being successful with the investment. Is it worth putting your retirement dollars on the line for a 60% success rate? (See figure 2)

Figure 2

Investment Success % Calulation:

$$\frac{15 \text{ power Points}}{25 \text{ points "the Perfect Investment"}} = 60\%$$

By the use of the POWER points and the investment success percentage calculation, you can judge if this investment has a good probability of success before you invest. If you feel this investment is OK, you'll probably want to make a more thorough investigation of it to reassure yourself before you invest. Remember, let your financial common sense be your guide. "If it sounds to good to be true, it usually is!"

One final example. A sales person who specializes in retirement funds calls you. He begins his sales pitch on an Adjustable Rate U.S. Government Fund. Since this is of interest to you, you patiently listen. When the sales person is finished, you ask him if you can ask a few questions about the investment.

Before you start your inquiry, down the lefthand margin of a page write the word POWER with the numerical POWER points next to each letter. You are ready to inquire.

Investment: Adjustable-rate U.S. Government Funds

1. P-(*principal safe?*): You begin to ask, "Will this investment keep my principal safe from financial loss?" The sales person replies, "Since these funds will be invested in U.S. government agency mortgage-backed securities, they are very safe and will protect your principal." After his response, you give it 5 POWER points.

2. O-(*optimum cash flow*): "Does this investment produce income and if so how can I receive it as retirement?"He replies, "Are you familiar with adjustable rate home mortgages?" "Yes. If my understanding is correct, doesn't the interest paid on these loans vary every year?" The salesperson states, "Since this fund invests in U.S. Government-insured mortgages, the interest received will vary as interest rates fluctuate up or down. You may receive the interest earned either monthly, quarterly, semiannually, or once a year and still keep your principal intact." You say to yourself, "I need money monthly so I assign it 5 POWER points."

3. W-(*wealth builder?*): "How does this investment compare to inflation, and will it preserve my future purchasing power" He responds, "Since you seem to understand the effects of inflation, this investment will help protect your future purchasing power. If interest rates goes down, your fund flow will be reduced some. If interest rates go up, so will the return on your retirement funds. You know inflation this year is projected to be about 3-4 %. These funds

are currently paying 7-8%, which is approximately twice the rate of inflation." At the conclusion of his discussion you decide to score this portion 4 POWER points.

4. E-(*easily understood?*): You quickly say to yourself, I think I understand it, but I need more information on sales charges, etc. so I'll give this 3 POWER points.

5. R-(*risk/return percentage*): "Tell me once again, what is the lowest interest rate you think it will pay, and the highest?" "As we have discussed previously, since the Adjustable-rate U.S. Government Fund's interest rates move up and down, your return adjusts with the market. Currently the fund is paying 7-8% annually. But remember, if interest rates go higher, so will the fund's income. The investment and market risk is minimal, if any." You respond to yourself, The interest returns seem to be OK with the risk, I'll give it 5 POWER points.

6. *investment success percentage calculation:* Compute your Investment Success Percentage: 5 POWER points for *principle safe,* 5 POWER points for *optimum cash flow,* 4 POWER points for *wealth perserver,* 3 POWER points for *easily understood,* and 5 POWER points for the *risk/return percentage;* the total is 22 POWER points. Divide the 22 POWER points by the "perfect" investment points of 25 and the percentage result is 88%. This 88% indicates I may have a 88% chance of this investment being successful.

In these examples, you see how valuable the use of this financial formula can be to your future financial success. With the use of POWER points and the investment success percentage, you can more easily gauge, and with reasonable accuracy, which investment you are considering is right for your retirement funds.

The next chapter is titled, "The Deadly Deceptions," so turn and learn.

11

The Deadly Deceptions

Have you ever watched with amazement the skilled magician make seemingly large items appear and disappear right before your eyes? Magicians live by the ability to perfect these illusory deceptions that are so real that audiences tend to believe the magician has actually created a mystical event. The illusion is so believable, common discussion among its viewers would suggest it is reality rather than deception.

The investment community has its share of illusions also. Some are so believable that investors line up to place their hard-earned dollars in investments with features which are too good to be true.

Lets explore a few of these investment illusions.

Deception #1
Buy Only "No Load" Mutual Funds.

There are those who sincerely believe mutual fund companies, who boast of no load, actually manage your money because they are financially benevolent, with no profit incentive in their business plan. Their mission in life has the illusion of providing only public service to society.

Possibly we should look at the means used to build their office structures, pay rent, pay for advertisment, compensate executives, pay salesmen, or reward their masses of telephone solicitors.

The fuel that drives businesses is profit. They either make it or they fail in business.

No-load mutual-fund companies must also succumb to this most fatal disease, profit, or they too will cease to exist. Profit for mutual-fund companies is earned in several ways. It is either made by charging front-end fees called loads plus a moderate annual fee for its continuing service or it is made by charging an annual fee plus a deferred sales charge and a (12b-1) fee, for redemption of your money before the company has had the opportunity to earn sufficient annual management fees to reimburse itself for the costs involved in setting up your account and compensating the person who sold you the fund. This person may have been paid either a salary or a commission.

Lets look at the effects of a $10,000 initial investment for a front-end load fund and a no-load fund with identical performance.

Assumptions:

1. Front-end load 5%—Annual management factor 1/2%
2. No load—Annual Management factor 1½%
3. Initial investment $10,000
4. Investment period 10 years
5. Mutual funds are not intended to be trading vehicles
   A. The objective of your mutual fund should be to invest for the longer horizon (3 to 5 years or longer) and receive professional management of your funds.
6. The performance of each fund is identical, at 14% annually
   A. The fund is a stock (equity) fund.

The following illustration shows only the year-end results for the first 10- year investmenl period. The longer the illustration is projected, the more significant the result becomes. No allowance for taxes has been projected.

Year		Load	No-Load
Start		$10 000	$10,000
	Load	(500)	-0-
	Begin	9500	10,000
1		10,782	11,250
2		12,238	12,556
3		13,890	14,238
4		15,765	16,028
5		17,893	18,020
6		20,309	20,272
7		23,051	22,806
8		26,163	25,657
9		29,695	28,865
10		33,704	32,473

Much more important than the front-end load is the consistency of the management. You cannot buy past performance. That is history, never to be repeated in exactly the same form. You can however, buy the management which created the performance. If they did it once, can they do it again? It seems the likelihood of a repeat performance by an experienced, professional mutual fund company (team with the same players) over an extended period of time is a safer risk (bet) than putting your confidence in a company (team) with new or un-tested management (coach and players). Even a shift to a new set of economic circumstances (league) has an impact on the eventual result (score). The experienced company (coach and players) over the long term (many seasons) will be the more consistent investment (winners).

Deception #2
I Have My Social Security For Retirement

Will social security keep up with inflation? Some have speculated social security will increase at about 3% per year. If inflation increases at 5% per year, where will the 2% per year shrinkage come from, your living standard or your investments?

Deception #3
I Only Do Business With a Discount Broker

Why should I pay $60.00 commission when a discount broker will transact my orders for $39.95?

If you are able to study all the possibilities for your invested dollar and duplicate the research completed by major brokerage firms with their research staff of qualified, experienced analysts and establish a list of investments that will out—perform the investment markets with less risk about 7 out of 10 times, . . . a discount broker is for you.

Discount brokers are not allowed to perform investment consulting services for you. They are transaction specialists. You may call and give them your trading instructions. They will follow your instructions—end of relationship until your next investment instruction.

Deception #4

Take the Single Life Annuitization
on the Company Pension Plan

The monthly payment goes up. You can invest the difference and improve your monthly cash flow.

An acquaintance of ours followed his friend's advice. Indeed the monthly cash flow was better, until he died suddenly of a heart attack. Having elected the single life annuity rather than the joint and survivor lifetime income, his widow was left with no income other than social security for the rest or her life. The election, once made, is not subject to change if you discover you have made an error. To protect the survivor with lifetime income, weigh carefully the comfort of a joint lifetime income before taking the higher monthly amount on a single life.

Deception #5

Pay Your Taxes as They Accrue Yearly
So You Won't Have a Large Tax Bill When You Retire

The following chart illustrates the power of tax deferred compounding.

Client Name: Happy Camper   Assumptions:
Client's Age: 40   Constant Tax Rates
Age Projected To: 65   Lump-sum Withdrawal
Tax Rate: 35.00%   at Maturity
Initial Investment: $10,000
Interest Rate: 7.00%

Taxable Compounding		Tax Deferred Compounding		
Age	Interest	Balance	Interest	Balance
40		$10,000		$10,000
41	455	10,455	700	10,700
42	476	10,931	749	11,449
43	497	11,428	801	12,250
44	520	11,948	858	13,108
45	544	12,492	918	14,026
46	568	13,060	982	15,007
47	594	13,654	1,051	16,058
48	621	14,276	1,124	17,182
49	650	14,925	1,203	18,385
50	679	15,604	1,287	19,572
51	710	16,314	1,377	21,049
52	742	17,056	1,473	22,522
53	776	17,833	1,577	24,098
54	811	18,644	1,687	25,785
55	848	19,492	1,805	27,590
56	887	20,379	1,931	29,522
57	927	21,306	2,067	31,588
58	969	22,276	2,211	33,799
59	1,014	23,289	2,366	36,165
60	1,060	24,349	2,532	38,697
61	1,108	25,457	2,709	41,406
62	1,158	26,515	2,898	44,304
63	1,211	27,826	3,101	47,405
64	1,266	29,092	3,318	50,724
65	1,324	30,416	3,551	54,274

Future Value $54,274
Initial Investment -   10,000

Taxable Gain   44,274
Tax on Gain @   35.00%   15,496

                       28,778
Initial Investment +   10,000

After-tax Funds   After-tax Funds
Taxed Yearly $30.416   Tax Deferred $38,778

Notice on the chart if taxes are paid yearly, the amount available for retirement is $30,416. If taxes are deferred the after-tax amount available for retirement is $38,778. If the financial vehicle used to accomplish this increased amount is a tax deferred annuity, you would deduct your initial investment before calculating your taxes. The illustration assumes the entire account would be withdrawn at one time and taxed at the same rate as when the account value was being accumulated. Rarely would one pursue this approach. Withdrawals would ordinarily be received according to need. This would usually preserve the benefit of a lower tax rate on withdrawals.

If the projection is to measure the anticipated result of a retirement account or a 401(k) plan, taxes would be due on the entire account without deducting the initial investment as in the annuity illustration. Annuities would ordinarily be purchased with after-tax dollars. Qualified retirement accounts are accumlated with pre-tax dollars.

This same compounding effect happens whether you use tax deferred annuities IRA's, or the company profit-sharing 401(k) plan. When you defer taxes, you earn income on the portion which would ordinarily be due for taxes. The amount or yield earned on the portion which will at a future date be paid as taxes also earns interest. For example, $100 interest earned on the balance in your IRA account will some day have a tax due of about $35; however, sixty-five dollars of the interest earned on the account stays as a permanent asset in your tax-deferred account.

Deception #6
Never Pay a Premium For a Bond

Premium, in this context, refers to the amount you must pay for a bond over its face amount (usually $1,000). For example, a bond with a coupon of 9% may be selling at a premium of 5%. In other words, the price would be 105 or 105% of its face value. In the example used, the bond would cost $1,050 ($1,000 X 1.05). The $50 is the premium. The effect of this $50 premium is to lower the yield to about 8½%. In other words, you would have invested $1,050 to receive an annual cash flow of $90. Lets look at this illustration more closely.

Coupon	Face Value	Purchase Price	Cash Flow	Yield
9%	$1,000	$1,050	$90	8.57%
8%	$1,000	$1,000	$80	8.00%
7%	$1,000	$ 950	$70	7.37%

In the illustration, one may be duped into believing that buying a bond at a discount is like buying it on sale. Not so! The price paid for the bond and the terminology of discount and premium refers only to the price, not to its value. Value is a measurement of yield in relationship to yields available in the market for bonds of similar quality and maturity. There is an inverse relationship between price and yield. If the price goes up, the yield goes down. If the price goes down, the yield goes up. The following chart may illustrate this more clearly.

Coupon %	Maturity	Face Value	Price	Cash Flow	Yield %
8%	2005	$1,000	$105	$80	7.62%
8%	2005	$1,000	$100	$80	8.00%
8%	2005	$1,000	$ 95	$80	8.42%

Notice in the illustration, the fewer dollars invested, the higher the yield. In other words, if you invest $950 and receive a cash flow of $80, this is a higher yield than if you had invested $1,050 for the same cash flow.

Please refer to the chapter on the Top Ten Investment Parade for a more detailed discussion on bonds.

Deception #7
I Time the Market

When the market goes down I am in cash. When the market bottoms, I reinvest and ride the market back up.

To our knowledge there has never been a long-term successful market timer. The people who believe in the philosophy of market timing for their investments are most often chasing yesterday's heros. If it were possible to accurately and repeatedly forecast where the market was going, everyone would jump on the band wagon and there would be no market. It would be a given that under certain circumstances the economy would react a certain way and the proper action would always be dictated.

The local, national, and world economies are a fish bowl of the past for all financial gurus to pontificate over, speculate on and convince the world they know what is going to happen in the future. At best we can only speculate that current circumstances, when impacted by actions based on the past will react in a similar manner in the future.

Deception #8
This Is a Guaranteed Return on Your Capital

Who issues the guarantee? In the past a common sales pitch has been to refer to a guarantee. For example: no one has ever lost a dime in insurance in the history of the United States. Possibly true until 1990 when several insurance companies were declared insolvent and taken over by insurance commissioners under a conservatorship arrangement. It remains to be seen whether or not the policy holders will indeed receive their expected insurance benefits.

In some cases Universal life insurers were "issuing guarantees" of 14% return for a specified period of time. Who guaranteed this return? The insurance company who issued the commitment to pay the 14%. In one sense, this is like receiving a guarantee for security on the hen house, signed by R. Fox. Remember, a guarantee is no stronger than its issuer.

How can insurance companies pay 14% to you as an investor? They must earn a return greater than 14% so they can meet their operating expenses and also satisfy their owners. How do they earn 16% + on their investments?—Right, junk bonds or other high risk investments.

Remember the discussion on risk and reward? The higher the reward, the higher the risk. Yes, it is one of nature's immutable laws.

Deception #9
Art, China, Real Estate, and Collectibles Always Outperform the Market

Possibly, in the pure sense, because of the scarce nature of rare items and collectibles and to some degree real estate, the actual value does increase dramatically. The problem for the average person who someday may need to liquidate the assets to enjoy the benefits of relaxed retirement is that the items may be hard to convert to cash. Who is going to buy the rare items of china or collectibles? If the right buyer can be found, the real asset value may be realized, if not a sacrifice price is most often the result for a person who needs liquidity and does not have time to wait for proper market conditions and the right buyer.

A person who invests in assets of this type should do so because of the enjoyment factor rather than an anticipation of liquidating them at his or her convenience for a profit at some future date.

Deception #10
"Our Investment Has averaged 16% Over the Past Ten Years"

Invest now and begin to immediately reap these rewards. Look at our performance chart.

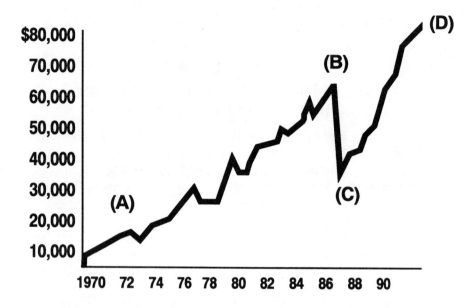

The real question is where are we on the chart, or, where are we in the investment cycle? If we are at point A heading for point D, that may be a tolerable performance. However, if we are at point B heading for point D, this is a heart-attack journey.

Be sure your investment is positioned to best fulfill your investment objective. Be careful of the investment with a twenty-year time horizon if you plan to retire in three years.

the price and thrill of the ride:

Trip	Result	Price
A to B	Wonderful	A steal
A to D	Enjoyable	Bargain
A to C	Tolerable	Fair
B to C	Heart Attack	Very heavy

Please refer to the chapter on the Top Ten Investment Parade for a more detailed discussion of investment objectives.

Deception #11
I Can't Afford to Put Money Into the Company 401(k) Plan

The following illustration assumes a company match of your invested dollar is available and an employee tax-withholding rate of 15%. Many company sponsors match up to a certain limit of employee dollars deferred into the 401(k) plan. Some sponsors do not. Check with your company benefits or human resources department for the specific benefits of your plan.

Payroll	$1,000	
Deferral	$ 70	7% Employee Deferral
Tax Saving	$ 15.40	15% Federal 7% State
Net Cash Decrease	$ 54.60	Deferral, less tax saved
Company Match	$ 17.50	Assumes 25% match by employer
Profit Realized	$ 32.90	Tax saved plus match

In our illustration, you, the employee, earn $1,000 gross income. You decide to defer $70 into the company 401(k) plan. Since this $70 is not taxed you have an immediate cash-flow savings on your pay check of $15.40. You have experienced a net cash-flow decrease on your check of only $54.60. As explained above, your company may match a portion of your deferral with a company contribution to your future retirement benefit, called a company match.

By combining your tax saving of $15.40 together with the company match of $17.50, you have a benefit of $32.90. A $32.90 gain on a saving amount of $70 is an immediate gain of 47%. We would recommend any time you can get a no risk gain of 47%, take your money and run.

Deception #12
Squeeze the Last Dollar Out of Your Investment Gain

If you decide a target price for your investment at its inception, sell at the target price. One of the wisest and richest men to have acquired his wealth from investments was Bernard Baruch. When asked how he made all his money in the stock market he replied, "I sold everything too soon."

If the basics upon which you based your decision to invest change, and the indicators seem to tell you to sell, don't place your sell order at a price above current trading prices with the anticipation that your patience will benefit you while waiting for the market price to come to your sell order price. If it is time to sell, sell! While you are waiting for the last 1/8 point raise in the price you may experience a continually deteriorating price in the market. You will probably wish you had sold rather than waiting for the last bit of profit.

In the next chapter, we will take you on a true life adventure in the world of finance titled. "To Be Or Not To Be."

12

To Be Or Not To Be

To be or not to be retired, comfortably—that is the question. Who has the control of your future retirement status? You. No one else.

We were counseling a couple about trying to make their $2,000-a-month income equal their $3,000 a month appetite. Needless to say, it didn't.

We explained the husband's options to get the outgo and income to match. After he disagreed with all the options, we related the final choice, "If you acquire other employment which will help your income needs and provide future retirement benefits, you'll do just fine."

He and his wife listened carefully as we outlined the success plan for him to meet his $3,000 financial need. The solution was simple, but as he departed, his "success drive" was in need of repair.

Your Attitude Determines Your Retirement Altitude

Which reminds us of a story in the Bible—when the people of Israel were being wicked, and the Lord caused fiery serpents to go among them to inflict pain, suffering, and even death. The Lord instructed Moses to make a pole with a fiery serpent made of brass to be placed on the top of it. He further instructed Moses to tell the people if they will have faith to look upon the brass serpent, they would be healed and live. The story continues that many didn't look upon the fiery brass serpent and died. (Numbers 21: 5-9)

How easy would it have been for them to simply lift their head and look at the fiery serpent made of brass to be healed? How easy could it have been for the husband to get up and get going to be successful?

There is another famous story from the Bible about Naaman the Syrian, captain of the host of the King of Syria. He was a great and honorable man. He was a mighty man in valour, but he had leprosy. He called upon Elisha the prophet for healing. Naaman was expecting some grand-slam miracle as he waited outside the house of Elisha. We're sure Naaman was thinking of some unusual, unique, once-in-a-lifetime healing deal.

When Elisha's messenger arrived to give Naaman Elisha's healing instructions, the messenger told Naaman to go to the river Jordan and wash himself seven times, and "thy flesh shall come again to thee, and thou shalt be clean."

Naaman was greatly displeased! After that his servants gave him some good advice, which simply stated was "Do it." The captain swallowed his pride as he looked at his diseased body and followed the simple and easy instructions of Elisha's messenger. After the seventh washing in the river Jordan, "his flesh came again like unto the flesh of a little child, and he was clean." He repented before Elisha for his negative attitude. How simple the instructions, and how great the life saving result. (2 Kings 5: 9-15)

Someone said quite unjustly, "If it isn't complicated don't believe it." Quite the reverse is true. The simpler the better. Remember the old KISS Formula. Keep It Simple, Stupid. This also applies in building, preserving, and accomplishing your retirement goals.

We believe there is very little difference in people. But that little difference makes a very big difference. The little difference that makes a big difference is your attitude. We believe attitude determines in large measure your financial retirement altitude.

At a recent conference, a famous person was speaking about education to a vast audience. At the conclusion of the meeting, a student came up and said, "I want you to give me the secret to be successful in school." The kind learned man thought for a few seconds and counseled, "Your grades are not reflective of your aptitude, but your attitude." The future young scholar walked away bewildered at the learned man's advice.

There is no such thing as a free lunch. If you are going to retire right, then plan right, with the right attitude. Only 5% of the people ever plan for a result. Be in the top 5% and be a retired winner with an RFC Degree! That is a *Retired First Class* Degree.

We believe you can have anything in life you want as long as you plan for it properly with enough time and work. Remember these most important words: *plan, time,* and *work!* Retirement doesn't work unless you do.

We can hear some of you saying, "Sounds too easy to be true." Let's hear from two people who planned, worked, and achieved retiring first class. Their stories are true and illustrate that you too can have a very successful retirement.

In our first story on retiring first class, we meet Jim and Jane (not really their names). The story and description of achieving their retirement is true, as described by Jim.

A Dream Come True

The first twenty-one years of my life were the hardest times one probably could face. During this time of my life I worked in a saw mill for 75 cents a day. After that the coal mines paid me not much more for two years. On my 19th birthday, I finally graduated from high school, and it was off to the Army for a while.

During my military stay I was injured in an automobile accident which placed me in a hospital in the beautiful Missouri Ozarks. It was also here, I met and married Jane, the best decision I ever made.

As the years went by, and we were in our early thirties. We moved to Texas with our only son, and I was hired by the railroad and started my long trek to retirement.

After securing employment, the next decision Jane and I had to make was where to live. After a long debate over our house payment, we purchased our first dream home made of adobe. It consisted of two bedrooms, a living room, kitchen, and one very small bathroom. The real estate agent said it was a steal at $11,000. But it was nice and was situated on one-and-a-half acres of land. We placed our life savings of $4,000 down, praying we could make the house payments each month. Little did we know then that this first home would be the most important investment we would ever make.

Upon completing the closing of our "mud hut," as we referred to it, I worked sixteen-hour days for many years to keep up with the expenses of the family and our homestead.

The years quickly passed. One day Jane called me at work very excited. She said, "Can you come home right away? Something marvelous has happened to our son."

"What is it?" I asked. "Come home. You won't believe it until you see it," she replied most anxiously.

As I drove home , I wondered what this exciting news could be. Little did I realize what the good news was until I heard it from my son.

"Dad," my son exclaimed, "I just got a four-year scholarship, all expenses paid, to play football and track. Isn't that great?"

Suddenly, tears began streaming down my cheeks as I recalled how many years before, in a very serious financial meeting, we told our son we wouldn't be able to afford college for him, and he would have to work or make do on his on. It was one of the hardest decisions my wife and I have ever made. You see, no one in our family has ever graduated from college and this news could change all of that.

"Dad, isn't that great?"

"It's not only great, but think of all the money we will save on your food bill," I humorously and tearfully responded. That day was a great blessing to our family and our son.

After he was off to college, Congress, believe it or not, decided to pass a bill that made IRA's possible. About the time this bill was passed, we really started thinking seriously about being 65, and about our future retirement.

We realized if we made IRA contributions, this would help us build our retirement nest egg. In order to buy another home mortgage free, we decided to remodel our home. We felt that this would increase the value of our property. When the house would sell, the sale proceeds would provide a debt-free retirement home for us in the good old Missouri Ozarks. We spent approximately $2,000 on our remodeling and added here and there, particularly in the bathroom. At the time of all these decisions, we were about twenty years from retirement.

As our son graduated from college and got married, time seemed to fly by swiftly. We decided to sell our "mud hut." We sold it for $45,000 with 29% down and the balance on an installment contract at 7%. Payments of $400 a month including principal and interest would be paid. The buyer could not prepay the loan. He had to make the payments for over 16 years. The total proceeds to us would be in excess of $100,000, and the buyer agreed to such a deal. Our nest egg for retirement began.

After selling our home, we purchased for cash a mobile home for $15,000, and our savings was really growing.

The second year after the law authorized IRA's, we made the maximum contributions allowable each year. We felt with the sale proceeds from the house, our IRA deposits each year, and our savings invested wisely, we would have a good retirement.

Meanwhile, of course, I continued to work hard on the railroad, and my retirement benefits were building as well. As I worked, we managed our money and poured our savings into the bank and invested them.

After 32 years of working on the railroad, my retirement date arrived. It was sad to leave, but we were looking forward to the new era of our lives.

The first thing we did was sell the mobile home. We sold it for $15,000, the exact price we paid for it years before. The proceeds from the sale of our first home were in the bank accumulating interest. Our IRA's were worth a lot, and our investments were growing. Our retirement benefit from the railroad exceeded $2,000 a month. All in all, the savings and budgeting were about to pay off.

We designed and built our dream home in the Missouri Ozarks on six acres of land, across the street from a golf course. Wouldn't you know it, we don't play golf, but we will learn.

We paid cash for the our home, the six acres, the little red barn, and tool shed out back. It took about a year for our new brick home with all the modern trimmings including landscaping to be completed. We still save money from our retirement checks each month—a habit we learned many years before. The most difficult decisions we have to make is where do we renew our jumbo CD's, and where do we fish today?

When we were in our early 20's, if someone would have told us this dream was possible, we would have told them "no way." But as we worked at it, it really seemed possible, then probable, then achievable, and then it happened.

We travel and spend most of our retirement time in community service helping other senior citizens. We fish. We hunt. Jane loves to play bingo and wins most of the time. At the senior citizen's home, I've sharpened up my pool skills and enjoy competing with our newly acquired friends. But most important of all, we are enjoying ourselves and each other.

If it wasn't for our planning, saving, budgeting our money, and thinking when we were a little younger of how we wanted to be when we got older, I don't feel we would have had a very successful retirement.

Believe you me, it was hard as we think about it now, but when I hear Jane shout out "Bingo" and win the prize, it was all worth it.

The Simple Life

Our second story is about the retirement of John and Marsha, as we will call them. The story is related by Marsha:

Now that we are retired, it feels good. But when we were 25 and had two children and were living on a small farm, the thoughts of retiring never entered our heads. We thought we were going to live forever, and life was wonderful.

As time went by, we sold our farm and moved to a larger town near by. We were then in our late thirties and had seven children, four boys and three girls.

Suddenly it seemed we were surviving one crisis only to be faced with another. Certainly now was not the time to be worrying about retirement. But we enjoyed the children and watched our little family, now a bigger family, gain maturity.

With the normal growth of a large family, expenses were increasing, so to help out, I took a job with the government. I soon learned a working mother never gets enough sleep, but my frequent naps at the dinner table or at church meetings seemed to help.

The routine of our family was set every day. My husband was off to work early each morning. My day started at 4 a.m. to get all the things done before work at 7 a.m. However, the children all pitched in and helped each day to make my working mom transition easier.

As time went by and as each of the children got older, we started to save a little money towards the future. Each of our employments had good retirement benefits, and we saved a little on top of that. Soon the children were all gone, and we both continued to work.

We could see retirement in the future and made a few plans. I started saving scraps of cloth for all the quilts I was going to make. I collected recipes for all the goodies I would bake. I put away books and articles I would read, and I dreamed of places I would visit.

My husband dreamed of all the animals he would raise and the very large barn to house the horses.

About ten years before our retirement, my husband came home with some house plans for our newly acquired 19 acres of land.

"Look" he said, "Our own log house. What do you think?" The plans were beautiful, but I said, "We can't afford it, can we?"

"Of course we can. We will have all four of our sons help us build the house. It may take us a while, but we'll get it done."

Seven years later, our dream home came true as we stood outside our beautiful 3,500-square-foot log home. It was a monument to our family. It was nestled beautifully in the middle of a meadow, over-looking a vast mountain range. We both would get that incredible feeling, as the sun would set every evening how lucky we really were.

As the years have passed, we have added grandchildren and various kinds of animals. Now I really can understand how Noah's wife must have felt in the ark. My husband is in his glory. And we are happy.

So now both of us are retired and enjoying it. I make quilts out of the material I've saved. I cook when family or friends arrive, which happens frequently. I read, ponder, pray in thankfulness. And when I get a chance, I go places. Why, I've even been to Greece with one of my daughters. And to top it off, I've been to Hawaii with my daughter and her husband with their eight children. We had a wonderful time.

When we retired, we still owed a good amount on our mortgage, but in the next few years, by managing our retirement incomes, we will have our loan fully paid and then our lovely home will be ours for keeps.

Sometimes retirement is a lonely life, but when I look at our half-acre garden in bloom, or the setting of the sun, or the grand-children on the horses riding and laughing, or when my newest blonde-haired, blue-eyed grandson Cody arrives, I know that our retirement is a blessing.

A good retirement isn't impossible as these couples realized. It is very possible with enough *planning, time,* and *work.*

In our next chapter, it's all up to you: you can do it!

13

Now It's Up To You— You Can Do It!

An interesting article came across our desk concerning retirement. The article stated some startling facts about future and current retirees. It revealed that 75% of the people who are working towards retirement or who are already in retirement are worried they will outlive their income stream. It continued to say, 73% feel they will need long-term health care which could erode their total life savings! The article also revealed that, 63% feared they would have to lower their standard of living in order to exist after a lifetime of hard work.

Another interesting retirement study we read stated that of 100 people who where studied from age 25 to their retirement age of 65, the following facts were unveiled:

1. Of the original 100 people, 29 of them had died before age 65.

2. Of the remaining 71 who were alive at age 65, 13 had a retirement income of less than $4,000 a year.

3. Of the remaining 58 who were alive at age 65, 55 of those people had median retirement incomes of $6,000 a year.

4. Of the remaining 3 people, only these 3 had an independent retirement source of over $26,000 a year! Can you believe it—only 3 out of the original 100!

Regardless of how you may feel about the results of the studies presented, retirement is coming, regardless of your age, and preparation is mandatory.

As we close the final chapter of this illuminating retirement volume, what should you have learned? Let's suggest a few final financial thoughts.

First, you learned, *People never plan to fail. They just fail to plan.*
You can have everything and anything you want in life now and in
the future, if you plan for it properly with enough time and work.
Retirement does not work unless *you do!* We illustrated for you some
excellent financial examples to help motivate you to start thinking
about your retirement, NOW.

Second, we discussed *budgeting.* A few years ago we hired a focus
group to replace the word budget with some other more-positive-
sounding word so people would be motivated to manage their money.
We flew a large group of people, who composed the focus group,
to Denver, Colorado. We paid for all of their expenses for one week.
Just imagine—for five days these very intelligent focus-group people
were to create, think, and replace the word budget with some other
word, preferably a word with more than four letters which we could
repeat to the public.

We will never forget the telephone call we received a few days prior
to their concluding meeting. As we answered the telephone call, the
director of the focus group said, "We feel we have the word you need.
Can you be here tomorrow at one o'clock?"

We responded with an enthusiastic, "Yes!"

Flying over the beautiful Rocky Mountains is a spectacular sight
indeed, but our minds were focused on the focus group's answer.
What would it be?

We arrived at the hotel and entered the meeting room. The focus
group's director stood, welcomed us and said, "We have found the
right word to describe budgeting." Has your heart ever raced while
you waited in anticipation for something? Now you know how we felt.

He continued, "The word is *budget.*"

"*Budget!,*" We exclaimed. "Did you say, budget?"

We continued," We flew you all here, paid in excess of $10,000
which is $1,666.66 a letter, and all you have to say is BUDGET?"

As the discussion continued, the focus group reiterated that budget
was the right word. The director of the focus group stated, "When
a person is not living within his or her income, budgeting is a negative

experience, and he/she will stop. However, when a person uses a budget and lives within their income, budgeting is a very, and we stress, a *very* positive experience, and he/she will continue. We know this is not the word you wanted, but the best word to describe a budget is BUDGET."

He continued, "Budgeting, you see, generates either a positive or a negative *feeling.* If you live within your income and save, the feeling is very positive and motivating to continue to be successful. And if you don't you won't continue. It is just as simple as that."

Needless to say, the focus group was absolutely right.

To prepare for retirement, you must manage your money, live within your income, and save 10% of your gross income each and every month. When you achieve your retirement goals, you will be fully prepared to manage your golden stream of income if you start budgeting your money now.

Thirdly, we illustrated for you the great financial benefits of *compounded interest,* and how its "offspring" will assist you in accomplishing your retirement goals. When you combine compounded interest with the use of the George Thomas Financial Rule, you will be able to compute the result and rest assured that compounded interest is positively impacting your retirement nest egg.

Fourth, we suggested various investments for your consideration, the use of the *investment pyramid,* and illustrated the use of the *financial "Power" formula sheet.* By using these financial tools, your retirement will be a happy one.

Lastly, we related to you true stories of people who actually used the facts in this book to insure their retirement. Their stories are heart warming indeed. As they revealed their financial adventures to us, we could see and feel all wasn't easy, but as they persevered and visualized their retirement goals, those goals became self-fulfilling.

We'll never forget the look on one grandmother's face when she described her blonde-haired, blued-eyed grandson's visits to her beautiful retirement home. Another couple, after relating their retirement story to us, took us on a guided tour of their newly constructed retirement home complete with over five acres of land all paid in full.

As the other couple related their positive retirement story, you could feel the great sense of confidence about their financial future which was built upon the financial disciplines of their past. It truly was a glorious experience to hear such motivating stories.

Their accounts clearly show everyone can have a great retirement, if they will plan and work for it. We read a great quote; it is, "In all thy getting, get going."

Their stories should illustrate to you the need to use a combination of these financial tools we have presented for you. By combining all of these ideas, your retirement will be as successful as theirs.

Let our final comments to you be, as you start on your successful road of *building, preserving,* and *enjoying* your retirement these immortal words:

NOW IS THE TIME

THIS IS THE PLACE

YOU ARE THE ONE

We wish you the best of success in RETIRING FIRST CLASS.

14

If You Need Help

1. If you need money management assistance call our national
MONEY MANAGEMENT HOTLINE:

801-625-1599

1-800-453-9408

2. If you want information on our corporate or individual seminars
on:

RETIRING FIRST CLASS

RICH ON ANY INCOME

Call our national SEMINAR HOTLINE: 1-801-625-1599

3. If you would like more detailed budgeting assistance, please call:

RICH ON ANY INCOME

at

1-801-625-1599

4. If you are interested in obtaining a RETIRING FIRST CLASS
AND RICH ON ANY INCOME franchise in your state, please call:

801-625-1599

15

Appendix

Your Investment Pyramid Outline
Your Financial POWER Formula Outline

This appendix contains your investment pyramid described in Chapter 6, and your very own financial "POWER" formula sheet discussed in Chapter 10.

Your Investment Pyramid

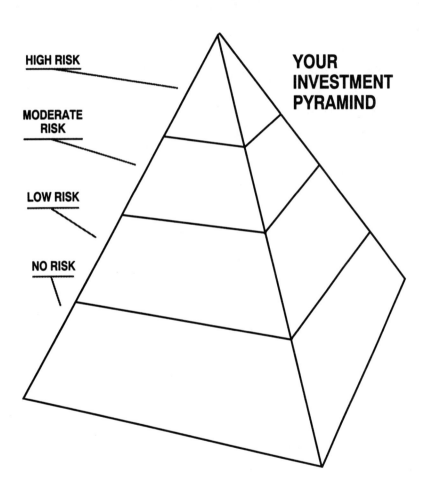

Your Financial POWER Formula

Investment Considering: _____

P   (Principle Safe): POWER points: _____

O   (Optimum Cash Flow): POWER points: _____

W   (Wealth Preserver): POWER points: _____

E   (Easily Understood): POWER points: _____

R   (Risk/Return Percentage): POWER points: _____

Summary Power Points:

P = _____ POWER points
O = _____ POWER points
W = _____ POWER points
E = _____ POWER points
R = _____ POWER points
_____ Total POWER points

Calculation of your *Investment Success Percentage* (ISP)

YOUR TOTAL POWER points: _____

_____ = _____ % : (ISP)

DIVIDED BY 25 (Possible Points)

Conclusion:

My chances of this investment being successful for my retirement is _____ % (ISP). Is it worth it? (YES) _____ or (NO) _____

INDEX

S

Shifting into retirement, 87
Single life annuitization, 112
Social change, 101
Social Security, 12, 111
Social Security check, 98
Spendable monthly income, 22
Spending categories, 22
Spending binge, 13
Spending habits, 12
Sports, 92
Standard & Poors, 70

T

Tax-free income, 46
Tax free, 17
Tax-equivalent yield, 72
Tax-deferred annuities, 17, 46, 49, 73
Tax-deferred, 42, 44
Travel, 93
Treasuries, 67
Treasury Instruments, 67
Treasury Bills, 55
Treasury securities, 49

U

U.S. Government funds, 107
Use of credit, 12
Utility stocks, 50

V

Value of money, 12
Variable annuities, 50, 74